Over the Edge Into Truth

Corey, God Bless you on your journey.

Paul Jensen

Paul Jensen
with *Todd Hillard*

insight
PUBLISHING GROUP

Tulsa, Oklahoma

OVER THE EDGE INTO TRUTH
© 2008 by Paul Jensen

Published by Insight Publishing Group
8801 S. Yale, Suite 410
Tulsa, OK 74137
918-493-1718

First Printing

Except where indicated, all Scripture quotations are from *The New International Version* (Grand Rapids: Zondervan, 1973). © The New York International Bible Society, 1978.

Used by Permission.

ISBN 1-932503-75-7
ISBN 978-1-932503-75-3
Library of Congress catalog card number: 2008923221

Printed in the United States of America

Dedication

To my wife Tiffany,
You have stood faithfully by my side and showed me how to be a better man.

To my children Jake and Audrey,
You are my joy and it is an honor to be your father.

To God,
You gave me a second life although I did not deserve it.
You forgave my sins when there were many.
You never left me when I left You.
I thank You for Your mercy, and may this book honor You.

Contents

All I want is reality. Show me God. Tell me what He is really like. Help me to understand why life is the way it is and how I can experience it more fully and with greater joy. I don't want empty promises. I want the real thing. And I'll go wherever I find that truth system.[1]

—Lisa Baker, age 20

Chapter 1

Miracle at Joshua Tree

Simon, Simon, be warned, Satan has demanded permission to test you and break you. But I have prayed that your faith may not fail. After you return to Me, I want you to give courage and strength to your brothers.
—Jesus Christ (Luke 22:31-32, THV)

Of all that is written, I love only what a person has written with his own blood.'
—Friedrich Nietzsche

Deep in the Southern California desert lays a large pile of rocks that rise out of the lonely sands, standing in defiance against the pounding of the sun and the relentless change of the seasons. Those who visit this place know intuitively that they don't belong; they walk as strangers in a strange land. It's a forbidding place; a place to drift for a couple of hours, or maybe a day or two before leaving, thankful that they don't have to make it their home. Those who come and go and think about where they have been depart with an uncertain feeling, not entirely sure they haven't accidentally trespassed—having passed through a place where they were never welcomed, a space where they didn't belong.

Joshua Tree National Park (as the pile of rocks is referred to today) strikes me as a place of leftovers—a dump of sorts—as if God haphazardly tossed piles of extra stone in the middle of this nowhere place; discarding them after He had constructed with care the mountains and valleys of the rest of the world. Even so, a certain beauty emerges from the desert floor in this place—but it is a beauty quite unlike any other. I've traveled the world and Joshua Tree looks like none of it; stark, barren, quiet, forsaken… a place where memories were abandoned long ago.

I find no mystery in the fact that humanity seeks to find itself in empty places such as this. We are instinctively drawn to raw spaces in search of ourselves or deep encounters with God who made us. With our lives now lost in an inescapable maze of instant messaging, cell phones, and the constant bombardment of media images from the most remote, bloodied, and broken corners of our world—is it any surprise that something in the innermost part of the soul beckons us to the quiet? It is so hard to see God when you are caught in six lanes of gridlocked traffic. It is so hard *not* to see God in the fading rays of a sunset over the desert. His presence is so obvious in the midst of the things He created… even in this random pile of boulders in Southern California.

In my life, I've left footprints in Joshua Tree three times, each visit transforming the contour of my life in completely different ways. Three short visits, each used by the One who created it to alter who I was to become—and am becoming—for eternity. It has never been a place to dwell, but more of a flash point, a point of contact, a place of impact that forever changes the course of my destiny even as the rocks themselves remain eternally unaffected.

The first time I laid eyes on Joshua Tree I was nearing the end of childhood—those obscure years between 6th and 8th grade. That season of life was highlighted by church camps and retreats where I had deeply connected with God. I was innocent; unadulterated by the darker side of the world. Life was good. The days were simple.

My first visit to Joshua Tree, however, was to mark the beginning of the end of such innocence. In the summer before my junior year of high school my family moved to a different state, seriously rattling my sense of stability. Desperate for the acceptance of new friends, I descended into a world where I allowed temptation and desire to quietly descend on my soul. At first ignorantly, and then with conscious abandon, I began to wander in the labyrinth of the world, with all its lies and deceit. Behind me lay the purity and simplicity of adolescent faith. Ahead lay a decade of twists and turns as I chased nearly every conceivable pleasure and pursuit.

In a vacuum constraint, my journey down this new found path accelerated during the years at college. Everything was more intense, everything came faster, everything more often. In the classroom I soaked in humanism and materialism. At night I partied with reckless abandon, never thinking of the consequences, focusing only on "fun at all costs." I read philosophy books late into the night, my life being contorted by these new, profound, and enticing thoughts that bounced aimlessly in my hollow soul—an arrogant soul… my heart knowing only the strength of youth and none of the wisdom of age. In the company of the great philosophers I found words to sooth my conscience, justifying the creature I had become.

After college, I entered the "real world" with great pride and confidence, motivated by a fierce spirit of competition that spilled over into everything: athletics, motor sports, business, the gym… I had an obsession to achieve what the world held in high regard, wandering away from my deep connection with God. But my second visit to Joshua Tree, nearly twenty years after my first visit, would change all that.

◆　◆　◆

In April of 2002, my extended family met together in Palm Springs for vacation. My parents, my sister, Karen, her husband, Todd, and their two children came from the east. We flew in from Seattle, where I was working for Microsoft. With me came my two kids—

Jake, aged seven, and my daughter, Audrey, who was four—and a beautiful and faithful woman named Tiffany, my wife of ten years.

The years had not been easy on Tiffany. While her presence had a calming effect on many of the outward storms I created, I was far from the companion I had vowed to be the day we wed. For the past decade I had lingered comfortably between Christianity and complacency, the empty places being filled with work, sports, cars, travel, and alcohol. Only recently had I found myself on the edge of rediscovering my faith. I was beginning again with God, recapturing the peace and meaning I had known as a child. So perhaps it seemed logical to return to the place that represented the summation of my childhood belief… the place that marked the end of a great season of faith. My sister Karen remembers my decision to go back to Joshua Tree this way:

> *Nobody really wanted to go with Paul. I mean, why trade the pools and the air conditioning for the cactus and the blistering sun? But Paul was insistent and we all had learned not to fight his stubbornness. What Paul wanted, Paul got, one way or the other. And that day he wanted us all to go to Joshua Tree. He rallied us and we packed up the car for the one hour ride into the desert. We all agreed to go reluctantly—but also purposefully. We had been seeing some hope lately in Paul's spiritual life, and he seemed drawn back to Joshua Tree—almost as if he were retracing his steps in some way.*

Joshua Tree looked just as I had remembered it. Mountains of boulders, huge and small, jutted through the sands and towered above the scrub trees that had given the area its name. In the parking lot we gathered our gear and began to hike through the brush and cactus on a meandering trail toward a large rock outcropping. If anything was wrong at that point, none of us recognized it for what it might have been. Looking back, some of us recall feeling like something was a bit "off," but we hiked on unconcerned.

At the base of the rocks my son, Jake, and I broke off from the group to climb higher. Pulling ourselves from boulder to boulder we worked our way up the side of a cliff. It was easy, it was fun, and the view got better each time we climbed a little higher.

Down on the desert floor, however, my brother-in-law, Todd, was experiencing something entirely different. He remembers it vividly:

After Paul and Jake separated from the group, I climbed with Tiffany, Karen, and the kids onto a big flat rock about six feet high. It's hard to explain what happened next, but deep in my gut I was struck by a horrible feeling—a mixture of anxiety and fear that began to pulsate through my body. I thought something was wrong with me. It didn't seem spiritual or mental... it felt physical and terrible. I was scared. First I thought I was having a heart attack, then I thought of the kids—something was going to happen to the kids. All I could think was "Let's get these kids off this rock. Now!" I started yelling at Karen and Tiffany to get the kids down. My heart was beating; I was breathing hard; my mind was a blur of thoughts and emotions.

You need to understand that I'm never like this. I'm usually the calm one, the rational one. I'm the one with the PhD who teaches at a university, the one who tries to be solid. But here I was in the middle of the desert freaking out over nothing. Tiffany thought I was nuts. She and Karen started to make fun of me, calling me a "wimp," telling me to get over it. But I couldn't. Something was wrong, and for whatever reason, I could feel it...and the feeling was awful.

Even as we huddled together safe on the ground, the sense of danger remained intense. I felt compelled to pray for our protection. "Watch over us, Lord, watch over us..." But I didn't think about Paul and Jake, not until I looked up and saw Jake seventy-five feet above us. "Oh God," I thought, "Jake is going to fall…" and that's when I heard Paul shout.

Above the group huddled below, Jake and I had climbed boulder by boulder until we were high above the desert floor. On a large, flat rock, about ten feet by ten feet, we had stopped briefly to take in the desert panorama that stretched out before us. It was beautiful; this is what I had come for. Jake stood near the edge while I walked back to the face of the cliff behind; I wanted to look over the top of the next rock to see if we wanted to go higher. To get high enough to see over, I stepped up onto a rock that was about eighteen inches wide at the base and rose to a point two feet high. With one hand lightly bracing me against the cliff, I stood on the pointed rock and peered over the top of the next ledge. *Just a little too risky for my son,* I thought. So I took my hand away from the cliff and began to step down off the small rock. There was nothing to this; a small step down onto a solid rock platform…

I have replayed the next events in my mind hundreds of times, each time trying to sort through the circumstances, trying to evaluate what happened, searching for some sort of natural explanation. But when I replay the details of those few fateful moments, earthly reason fails to explain what transpired.

As I made the small step down off the pointed rock, something moved, something lifted, something pushed… and I found myself momentarily horizontal, four feet in the air, looking down at the small rock I had used as a step. For an instant, my feet were at the same height as my head; for a fraction of a second time stood still as I lay parallel to the ground, suspended in mid-air. It was so surreally odd… incalculable. I remember thinking, *"How did I get here? I was standing on a rock two feet high and now my entire body is four feet off the ground."* As soon as I finished that thought, I dropped straight down, my hands hitting the ten by ten rock and my right knee striking the pointed rock I had been standing on. I shouted in pain. When I stood up I saw minor puncture wounds in both my hands; but more worrisome, was a gaping puncture under the knee cap. The cut went very deep and was bleeding badly.

I was in fairly bad shape and knew that I would need help to get my son down from the rock platform to the safety of the desert floor seventy-five feet below. Walking out four or five steps to the edge of the rock platform, I saw the huddled group below to my left. We had climbed up the right side as it was a gradual ascent. The left side however, was an extreme drop, and I was surprised to be looking nearly straight down onto the tops of my family's heads. I called down to Todd, asking him to help me get Jake down. Then, for whatever reason, I felt a little dizzy, so I backed clear away from the ledge, turned around, and put my hands on my knees. From this position, were I to pass out, I would have just fallen flat on the large flat rock, nearly six feet away from the edge. That's the last thing I remember. The memories of the others on the ground, however, are vivid and haunting. The images imbedded in their memories have allowed me to piece together the details of the next moments and hours—details which, like the pieces of a mosaic, give the full picture of what happened that day. Tiffany, my wife remembers this way:

I had been giving Todd a hard time about his fear. He was acting like a total baby, really wigged out. But when Paul called down from the edge of the cliff, my immediate attention turned to my son Jake. Was he all right? What was happening up there? Never, in my wildest dreams or my darkest nightmares could I have envisioned what I saw at that moment.

The whole world seemed to go into slow motion. Karen and I screamed; Todd turned and gasped... There, cart-wheeling slowly through the air, was Paul, his limp body twisting like a rag doll as he fell from the rock seventy-five feet above us. We lost sight of him a few feet before the point of impact, about thirty feet above our heads. The sound was awful, a hollow, deep thud... And then I heard nothing. I yelled at my son to stay put and began scrambling up the boulders, certain that I would find Paul dead. When I reached him, he was face down, his body twisted and distorted.

His right arm was contorted so far behind him that I thought it might have been torn off. The skin and scalp had been pulled away from about a quarter of his forehead, revealing the white of his skull. Dead? Alive? Dieing? I rolled him over. He breathed; I breathed, and somehow I knew it would be okay. I asked him to look at me, but his left eye was rolled so far back in his head all I could see was white. I asked him if he knew his name; he said "Paul." I asked him if he knew where he was; he said "Joshua Tree." I asked him to look at me and he kept saying "I am..." but his left eye never moved. The left side of his face was so bloody. I was terrified that so many parts of him were broken.

Karen, my sister, remembers the events this way:

Tiffany and I had bounded over the boulders like mountain goats and she got to Paul first. I remember wanting so badly to get to him—yet at the same time not wanting to get to him; so afraid of what I would find. To this day I don't like to think about it, actually. It was all so unreal. As soon as I got to him, Tiffany went up to get Jake to safety. I held Paul in my arms, and gazed into his eyes, but nothing looked back. My thoughts raced. He's not here. No, he's here, just unconscious. Is he still here? *In the confusion, however, one thing was very clear: I had never realized how much I loved him. As my brother, I had always taken him for granted; always letting the little things bug me... but not at that moment. I wrapped his mangled head in my shirt and held him in my arms, overwhelmed by my affections. As we sat, all I could say was "Jesus, Jesus, Jesus..." How much time went by as the two of us sat there alone? I have no idea. All I knew was that I loved my brother. All I could say was "Jesus, Jesus..."*

As Karen held me, I drifted in and out of consciousness. Tiffany had climbed up to get Jake and brought him back down to Karen and me. Karen then took Jake down to where the others were waiting, leaving Tiffany alone with me again. She assessed the situation this way:

The children were hysterical; crying, screaming. Our daughter kept yelling from the level ground below, "A snake bit Daddy! A snake bit Daddy!" Todd had already left to find help. I told Karen to get the kids out of there, which she did, leaving me alone with my husband. For a moment I was able to catch my breath and collect my thoughts.

Paul looked bad. Blood was everywhere. A large flap of skin had been peeled from his scalp. Veins and clumps of fat hung from the wounds. I tried to get him to look at me, but he said "I can't." I tried to keep him awake but he said "I don't want to." He kept saying "The wind was weird... I bonked my knee... Something pushed me... the wind was weird..." I look back at it all now and it all seems like a blur. Here I was, holding a horribly disfigured man, a man I loved, alone in this forbidden desert... and I had to wonder, "Was this my fault?"

Over the years I had been praying for Paul. He was such a bulldozer. He was a good guy, but he was totally out for himself. The kids and I were such a distant second—and God wasn't even in the picture. Our lives tumbled in the wake of his life. Soccer, work, cars, motorcycles, his friends... it was all about him and it was very difficult. My brother called him "an impossible nut to crack, a human superman..." I tried to get him to church, but it didn't take long to realize that I couldn't change him. So I turned to prayer. I prayed for three years that God would do something huge, because only something huge would work on

Paul. There had been small glimmers of hope, baby steps in the right direction; but as I held him in my arms, I wondered if this wasn't the huge thing I had prayed for—and I wondered if I wasn't somehow responsible.

Like the others, Todd jumped into immediate action. As he replays the event in his mind, these are the things he recalls:

Right after the fall, I ran for help. Because we were so remote, I thought the nearest help might be hours away. I was wrong. The people that God placed in the desert that day... it was miraculous. As I ran for the car, I found two climbers just beyond the next rock outcropping and yelled to them for help. One of them was a trauma surgeon who just "happened" to have a neck brace in his car. The other was a first responder with a backboard. In the nearest parking lot a rescue ranger with a van full of students had just pulled up. They had come to further their training in first-aid and wilderness rescue. Of the fifty people that "showed up" to help, thirty-five of them were medically trained. Tiffany said they just kept appearing out of the bushes. Many of the rescuers, however, were preparing us for the worst, using words like "brain damage, paralysis, internal bleeding, alive but not out of the woods." A group had gathered to pray at the base of the rocks where we had left the kids. The rescuers had formed a line from the accident site thirty feet up to a clearing down on the desert floor. A chain of people carefully lowered Paul off those rocks, taking him to the clearing where the helicopter picked him up.
As the dust settled, I waited behind to help clean up and fill out reports. I walked back to the cliff with a member of the rescue team, one who was well seasoned in Joshua Tree—and someone who knew the

consequences for those who fell there. He looked at the rocks with disbelief. "Drop one hundred people off of that," he said, "and one hundred will die." Together we were able to piece together the details of the fall: Paul had fallen from the ten by ten flat rock seventy-five feet above the desert floor, glanced off of two outcroppings and landed headfirst on solid rock forty-five feet below.

"...Drop one hundred people off of that and one hundred will die... one hundred will die..."

In the commotion I was left without a ride back to Palm Springs. I hitched a ride to the park entrance where we arranged for Karen to come back to pick me up. With two hours to wait and think, the events of the day began to settle in my mind—and certain unanswerable questions began to lead me to some unsettling conclusions. First, it made absolutely no sense that Paul should have fallen. Paul is an incredible athlete; an excellent soccer player, gifted football player, a weight lifter in perfect condition. Paul was a jock; tough, strong, and highly coordinated. That he would fall by accident in such an easy situation was unthinkable. Then there were the screams of his daughter, "A snake bit Daddy." What was I to make of that? She had no prior fear or awareness of snakes and none were seen or talked about that day.

Most disturbing, however, was the deep premonition of evil and fear that I had in the minutes before the fall. In the flurry of the rescue I hadn't had time to draw a connection between those two events. But now, with some time to put it all together, I realized that the very moment that I thought Jake was going to fall, Paul had unexplainably "slipped." I had to conclude that something happened up on the rock that day. I wasn't sure what, but something happened.

I wasn't sure of what had happened either. As I lay on the rocks, consciousness slowly returned, but it was like a fog retreating into the night. I began to hear, but wished I could not. I heard the screams of my four year old daughter: "Daddy's dead! A snake bit Daddy! My Daddy is dead!" It wasn't the standard scream of a young child, but a scream that pierces your soul. I listened to the voice of my wife, Tiffany, her words so shaken—holding back tears and offering uncertain comfort. My wife is very strong in emergencies, so when I heard the fear in her voice I knew I was in bad shape. "I'm here, Paul. I'm here…" she managed to say.

Her broken voice began to answer the questions of other voices—unfamiliar, professional, questioning type voices: "Let me look at him, Ma'am… Can you tell me how high? Paul, can you feel this?" I tried to look at the voices, but the visual world was a blur of painfully distorted images, and so I held them tightly shut. The number of voices continued to grow, punctuated now by the crackle of radios. I lay helplessly on the unforgiving rocks for hours. One moment I felt like I had died, then briefly brought back to life, only to feel myself sliding on a slope toward death again. I didn't want to leave my family; I didn't want my life to end at such a young age. Yet in the midst of all the chaos—in great defiance to the circumstances— a deep peace was felt in my soul—a *remarkable* peace. I felt my life's journey on this world was ending, that a new journey was about to begin, yet there was peace in the midst of confusion. It's hard to describe the feeling, but what a blessing it was in those hours.

Eventually I felt my body being carefully moved and lifted, followed by the cool sensation of metal against my back. I heard the sound of duct tape as my limbs and head were immobilized against the backboard. The voices began to carry me through the rocks. I sensed the movement and I saw shadows moving about me, but they didn't seem to match up with anything in my mind. My sight was returning slowly and as it did everything looked different. Even things that were familiar and recognizable seemed… different.

They gently placed me on the sand and many minutes passed as we waited for transport. Soon I heard the chop of blades cutting through the dry air, followed by a blast of dust and a new set of voices.

They loaded me up and Tiffany jumped in. As the ground fell away below us I felt a surge of disorientation, claustrophobia, and pain. My body tensed and heaved as we flew through the turbulent desert air, but the strange and powerful sense of calm that had descended on my heart continued. I can't explain it, but the peace was complete and it was nearly perfect.

As we landed at the hospital and entered the world of white coats and florescent lights, Tiffany had to face our uncertain future:

> *The helicopter flight was followed by a frantic series of tests at the hospital including X-rays and CT scans. That Paul was even alive seemed miraculous to me. Now I awaited the diagnosis as they finished cleaning his wounds and stapling him back together. As I sat beside his bed in the ER, a stream of doctors flowed in and out of the curtain. Some left shaking their heads; others were talking under their breath. Finally I had to ask what was going on.*
>
> *"Haven't you heard?" the doctor said. "He's known around here as 'Miracle Boy.' Listen, we have no idea what happened, but we know we aren't the only ones at work here. Your husband's tests have come back perfectly clear, all of them. Nothing, nothing, nothing. No broken bones, no fractures, no internal bleeding, The CT scan indicates that his brain hasn't even regis-tered trauma. You are welcome to stay in a guest bed tonight and we can observe him if you want, but your insurance isn't going to cover it, because there is nothing medically wrong with your husband."*
>
> *I could never put to words the emotions that flooded over me. How do you process something like that? It was all so overwhelming. What was I to make of the accident itself, let alone this news? The only injuries seemed to have come from the two times he glanced off the wall of the cliff. There appeared to be no*

damage at all from the force of the final impact. It was incredible!

While I was still in the ER I took a call from my mom. She had gotten a very brief message but she knew none of the details of the accident. "I don't know why," she said immediately, "But after Todd called, I started praying. I felt like Satan was trying to take Paul's life but God said, 'No, he is Mine.'"

After only 4 ½ hours in the hospital, we were released and went home.

◆　◆　◆

From this side of the grave, we will never know for absolute certain the spiritual details of that day. Time, however, has only reinforced in my mind a Scriptural interpretation of what took place. The final chapters of the Bible paint a picture of things evil and good, the conflict that exists between them, and how this clash is reflected in the events of earth—past, present, and future. The book of Revelation, in particular, presents graphic images of unseen spiritual realities that impact the domain of the physical:

And there was war in heaven, Michael and his angels waging war with the dragon... and the great dragon was thrown down, the serpent of old who is called the devil and Satan, who deceives the whole world; he was thrown down to earth, and his angels were thrown down with him... Woe to the earth and the sea, because the devil has come down to you, having great wrath, knowing that he has only a short time... So the dragon was enraged... and went off to make war against the rest of the children, who keep the commandments of God and hold to the testimony of Jesus.[2]

Had those who were in Joshua Tree been able to see into the spiritual realm that day, they would have seen an extension of this greater war. I believe they would have seen the angels of protection around us. I believe that they would have seen that protection temporarily withheld, that they would have seen Him allow a brief and limited assault by demonic forces. I believe they would have seen my feet being swept out from beneath me as I stepped down from the ledge, and moments later observed me being pushed from the heights by demons. And then, I believe they would have seen me being caught by angels of light on the surface of the rocks below. My brother-in-law sensed it. I think my daughter may have seen it. I'm certain my mother-in-law recognized it for what it was.

Time has also shown me some of the purposes of God in ordaining such things for my good... good that could only have come from something as dark as this. My life went over the edge that day, in so many ways. My body went over the edge physically, of course. But my soul was pushed over the edge as well, as my beliefs were awakened by the violent impact of the rocks. In deep and highly pragmatic ways, the fall catapulted me into a completely different paradigm for interpreting all of life, an entirely new way of seeing. The fall marked the beginning of a new season of transformation that has—and continues—to shape me into the man God created me to be as He now pushes me over the edge every moment of every day, conforming me to the image of His Son.

Why I was singled out to be specifically targeted by evil in this way, I'll never know. Why did God choose to save me, rather than end my life in the desert? I have no answer. The fact is that there is nothing special about me. The truth is that there is something special about *all* of us. We are each objects of the great love of God, targets of His attention and affections. As children of the One who is good, Satan has turned his wrath for the Most High toward us, "making war" against those God so deeply loves. The war is literal, not figurative. The enemy is real and tangible, not symbolic or metaphorical. And while the attack is individual, God's provision and protection is personal, allowing us to be wounded only for a greater healing.

At the end of the day, it's not a question about what happened to *me*. (Feel free to interpret my story as you wish.) The critical factor has to do with what is happening to *you*, and what you desire to see develop in *your* story. The Bible is very, very clear about the nature of the war, the war that encompasses everything around you and within you. The battles permeate the most significant areas of your existence, impacting the issues of faith, life, and love that matter the most.

Ultimately it's not about my story *or* your story. It's about *God's* story. To seek your story within His story is the beginning of a vital journey, a journey out of the personal desert common to all humanity. Each of us clings to an innate drive to understand the meaning of life. We yearn to make sense of pain and desire, hoping to get a chance to see "life" and "self" for what they are. The journey commences as we ponder God, stepping past current boundaries of perception and "seeing" everything that exists through new lenses—with eyes that recognize spiritual realities in the physical world. For when one begins to look at the world in this way—in a way that reflects both physical and spiritual realities—life will be truly pushed over the edge… but in all the *right* places, never to be the same again.

Chapter 2

See the World Clearly

Oh Lord, I pray, open his eyes that he
may see.

—2 Kings 6:17

L ife in the modern world moves to a certain beat; a cadence by
which the masses of humanity move around us. Sure, one might
think that he "marches to a different drummer," but the extent to
which that is possible is very limited. We all come into this world in
the same manner. We will all die as those who have gone before us.
In the in-between we sleep, work, and eat at predictable intervals,
breathing when we can, resting infrequently from the continual
demands. It all moves around us like a massive machine, a continual
drone of activity that propels us through in the perpetual currents of
society.

Or so it seems.

I was not so sure after Joshua Tree. I had thought I was aware.
I had thought I understood. But after the accident all was in question.
Thoughts swirled through my mind: *Perhaps there is a whole other
level of existence that encompasses and defines what truly is. Is life
as I have known it only an illusion, just a material mirage, or some-*

thing more tangible? Is it possible that what is seen and tasted and touched is only a shadow of true reality?

Such questions linger in the human soul. From time to time we might see images and impressions that give an instantaneous glimpse of the things beyond: the cry of a newborn, a dream of vivid proportions, the refraction of a sunbeam on a mountain lake, the cooling body of a loved one who has just "departed" for—for somewhere else. Unfortunately, such moments and the memory of them quickly pass, drowned out by the incessant drone and relentless demands of the "real world."

This begs a critical question: What if we've made a critical mistake in how we observe and interpret everything that's going on around us? What are the chances that we've made a fundamental error about the nature of life in general, a very basic error about how we envision life? What if what we *think* we see is not consistent with true reality? Maybe what happened that day in Joshua Tree wasn't a "miracle" at all. Maybe it was a glimpse of *true* reality, a snapshot of the world just beyond our view. A world we are destined for as well as the one in which we live...

A MATTER OF PERCEPTION

The human brain is a device of incredible complexity and capability. Its ability to manipulate physical data and input from the senses gives rise to the human mind. In the mind a matrix of thoughts and a paradigm of beliefs allow us to contemplate, imagine, and envision things beyond what the senses can tell us. In time, the mind develops what sociologists call a "worldview," an all encompassing mental perspective that determines not *what* we see, but *how* we see. The paradigm is the filter of all sensory input—signals of neural impulses that the mind translates into its own conceptual realities. Building upon previous mental constructs, the worldview morphs with experience and information, continually adjusting our perception of reality according to new sensory input.

Most of us don't even realize that we have a worldview, but we do; *everyone* does. It's an innate set of understandings and beliefs about what is real, how things work, and how life is organized, determining essential concepts of life such as family, the universe, self, and love. Our perceptions, in turn, determine our choices. Our choices, in turn, determine the course of our earthly lives—and even the destiny of our eternal lives. At the core of it all is our worldview.

In the Western world most of us hold to a worldview that divides up "self" into little compartments with specific contents in each:

- Career
- Education
- Faith/Religion
- Recreation/Hobbies
- Family/Friends
- Possessions/Finances

It is a clear reflection of the Western worldview that says our lives are made up of these things. When faced with options that appear to offer us a life that is meaningful and significant, the Westerner naturally focuses on each of the little pieces of the pie, thinking that if we fill each compartment, we will find what we are looking for. If our pursuit comes up empty, we usually conclude that we need *more*... more recreation, more education, and more money—*always* more money. That often requires a commitment of even more time and energy, further pushing us toward an emptiness of the soul. (Sometimes we might conclude that we actually need *less* of something to get a clear vision of what life is all about... less work, less possessions, less family hassles.)

This Western worldview also lends itself to the belief that "balance is the key." It's not always a matter of more or less; one of the keys to success is achieving everything in the right *proportion*. If you are having a hard time at work, maybe you need a little more recreation to tip the scale back in your favor. If you've had too much family lately, maybe you need to spend more "alone time" building up yourself.

This is the basic Western worldview of "self," and it's *powerful*. In fact, the mainstream media spends billions of dollars a year reinforcing this concept of life, because the business world knows that if you buy into this worldview you will buy a lot more of what they are selling. I know. I've been there. As a business executive for many leading companies, I've seen the influence corporations have. Throughout my life, I've traveled to over forty countries on five continents. I understand on a worldwide basis how the consumer thinks and how the marketers sell products, convincing people to buy things they may or may not need. For better and for worse, capitalism thrives on this simple fact.

Yet an even more fundamental division exists in the Western worldview of reality: *Westerners place a definitive line between the spiritual realm and the physical realm.* We make a clear differentiation between the physical things that can be seen and the spiritual things that seem to be beyond the grasp of our natural senses.

Spiritual:

- Soul
- Angels
- Ghosts
- Demons
- Discernment
- Morals
- Prayer

Physical:

- Health
- Home
- Work
- Education
- Religion (church, Bible study, etc)
- Family
- Possessions
- Recreation

This view of reality is based on the premise that a definitive distinction *can*, and *should*, be made between the things that are real (things we can touch and see) and the things of faith and the soul (which are unseen.) The barrier between the two realms is a boundary, a line, or an edge that must be transcended if something is to cross from one side to the other.

This two-part view of reality is a form of belief called "dualism." We hear echoes of dualism in our prayers when we ask that God would "come down" and "be with us" (a kind of spiritual "Red Rover, Red Rover, send God right over"). You hear it in the complacent agnostic who says that maybe there is a spiritual realm "out there," but how can anyone know for sure? You hear it in the cocky voice of the atheist who denies that the spiritual side exists at all. You hear it in our scientific skepticism that doubts that spiritual things can, or should, have any place in rational existence.

Most importantly, perhaps, is how this dualistic view of reality affects our pursuit of meaning and significance. It leaves us with the perception that if we want more meaning in our physical lives we need to cross *more often* into the spiritual side of things for *longer periods* of time. Those who have had their fill of religious things, however, will be inclined to search for more meaning in greater detail in the physical world (sports, recreation, drugs, etc) or pursue an ideology that is grounded in the physical.

Dualism also implies that God can be left behind as we go about our normal lives in the physical world—allowing us to leave things like demons and angels and miracles in a box in the spiritual realm as we live through our days in the physical realm with a sense of stability in material circumstances. Unfortunately, this view of reality assures us that any sort of supernatural experience is out of the ordinary, occurring only when things are out of their assigned realm.

Let me say this again: *The Western world view constructs in our minds a definitive barrier between the things of earth and the things of heaven, between the things of the flesh and the things of the spirit.* This perception affects everything. It affects work, relationships, and concepts of prayer and worship. It affects our expectations, our hopes, and our attitudes. Western dualism has tremendous rami-fications on our thinking and our attempts to make sense of life.

Don't be mistaken, unless one makes a conscious decision to analyze this worldview, they have no choice but to be driven by it. I should know. This worldview gave fuel to my professional career and it consumed my personal life. Nothing was fast enough, sensual enough, or extreme enough for me. In my pursuit of meaning and fulfillment I looked everywhere—in every compartment of "the pie." I looked for it in cars, women, drugs, work, motorcycles, intellectu-alism, and sports. I was (and to a lesser extent still am) one of the performers in this world. My natural instinct draws me into the outward things to fill vacant inward yearnings. Only through years of pain, suffering, perseverance, hope, and grace have I begun to conform my worldview to the mold that God intended.

Western dualism drives some into despair and countless others into survival mode. According to the A.C. Nielsen Co., the average American watches 28 hours of TV each week.¹ So what are we looking for or what are we trying to escape from? Many have found fragile contentment in a 9 to 5 job. Others drift into alcohol, drugs, or sexual experiences in hopes of drowning the pain by self-destructive behaviors that often push them even further from the realities of life.

If the essence of what we are looking for is to be found in the context of the Western worldview, certainly we should have discov-ered it. Never before has a generation been better equipped for the pursuit; no other generation even comes close to having the tools we hold in our hands. Consider this honestly: We have more information, we have more mobility, we have more discretionary time, and we have more money at our disposal than anyone else in history. We have instant access to vast amounts of information via the internet, satel-lite images show us every square foot of the planet, and aircraft can move us to any corner of the earth in less than a day.

Yet a quick inventory of our lives and the lives of those around us would indicate that we have missed it. Meaning, clarity, and signif-icance elude us. We search for it, we long for it, and we hope for the day when it will be ours. Our efforts and our passions fuel our desires for it. We seek it in the things we do, in the things we own, in the people we love. We seek it in adventure and in security and in power over others. We seek it through our career advancements, fine clothing, Botox injections, fake sun tans, new hairstyles, new cars, new homes, new "significant others," and other external adornments. We look desperately to the heavens for help and we scour the earth trying to find it.

Few of us lack zeal and commitment to find meaning and peace, yet our frustrations are compounded by the harsher realities of daily living. Most of life feels like a battle. We battle with the boss, with the spouse, with the kids, with the checkbook. Even from within us a battle rages. We struggle with temptation, with self-image, with shaken confidence, with unfulfilled hopes and dreams. We are left bruised, feeling empty, yearning for something more… even if it's nothing more than an explanation for why life is so tough.

While the things we desire generally elude us, from time to time we seem to find it, perhaps in the arms of a loved one, in a victory in the midst of a struggle, in the security of a little extra money in the bank. From time to time, we seem to grasp it—but then find that it dissipates with the setting of the sun. In the quiet of the evening, we wonder where the peace and meaning have gone. We had a taste of it; the taste did not satisfy long, and the hunger returns. It has passed us by again. Days can fade into months and months into years, and we wonder if we will ever find anything in lasting measure. As the years tick by, we wonder if there is anything out there at all.

As Henry David Thoreau stated so piercingly, "Most of us live lives of quiet desperation."[2] Perhaps that is the greatest struggle of all; the desperate, quiet struggle to find a sense of purpose, a sense of direction, a sense of meaning, and a sense of clarity. The struggle is to find a sense of *sense itself*—a desire to make sense of our world, where it's headed and what our part is in it. The Western worldview denies us of this desire, robs us of the hope of knowing that we count for a greater cause, that we are a part of something that is real and truly important, part of a process that makes a difference. Calling from deep in the soul cries a desire to be part of something bigger than ourselves. We hunt for anything that confirms our struggle is not in vain, that our efforts matter—*matter for something that in and of itself matters*—something worth dying for; making the grave more than an inevitable, anticlimactic end.

It's one thing to know you are in a fight. It's wholly different to know what you are fighting for, so let me ask the same question again: *What are the chances that we've made a fundamental error about the nature of life in general, a very basic error about how we envision life...one that is not consistent with true reality? What if we've made a critical mistake in how we look at and interpret everything that's going on around us on a deep level? Could that be the flaw that has thwarted our attempts on the surface level?*

LOOKING OVER THE EDGE

The "accident" in Joshua Tree forced me to see in different ways. The fall and the circumstances surrounding it were a "wake-up call" of huge proportions that literally and figuratively "rocked my world" and my worldview. The events of that day and the things that took place in the months and years that followed changed the way I looked at everything. I went through a complete paradigm shift—an altering of the mental matrix I was using to view the world. The initial transformations in my soul were vivid, graphic, and often laced with turmoil inside and out. The ongoing transformation has proved no less demanding.

> Stand at the crossroads and look; ask for the ancient paths, ask where the good way is, and walk in it, and you will find rest for your souls.
> —Jeremiah 6:16

I'm the kind that has learned most things the hard way; who by God's grace has survived and now thrives to live another day; one who is still on the journey, but has found the thing that had eluded me the most during my entire searching period: peace.

In my quest for acceptance by my peers, I forgot about peace. In everything I did, I sought success by the world's standards and I achieved it in great measure. But in each success, I found only emptiness. It took me years to realize that I liked to play soccer and race my motorcycle because it allowed me to forget about everything else. For a few moments of undistracted intensity, I could elude the haunting emptiness. When I was going 150 miles per hour racing other people, all I could do was focus on that instant in time or I would die. That focus provided me an adrenaline-filled moment of peace… but it was never lasting. Joshua Tree changed that. The accident, recovery, and everything I learned in the process finally revealed to me that all I was ever doing was looking for internal peace—a peace that comes from God alone, not from the physical world.

And such it is for so many of us. We search for peace but find only inner and outer conflict. We yearn for forgiveness and find only guilt, remorse, and fear—all tools of the devil that reinforce the Western worldview and destroy our joy and hope. Unaware of the freedom for which Christ came, we make it a duty to remember our sins, to hold onto the guilt, thinking it somehow makes us better; feeling that if we were to forget and be free, we would somehow be at fault, yet again. Oh, we have so distorted what God intended our lives to be. We strive to great ends to succeed, but with a worldview so contrary to His reality, our definition of success is in complete opposition to what God defines as success… the success that can only be found in what appeared to be the greatest failure of all history: Christ's death on the cross. This turns out to be the only place we can find the peace, the forgiveness, and the success for which we hunger.

I can tell you my story and I can show you what I've learned. But I cannot lead you or teach you. There are certain things that you must realize on your own, discoveries that only you can make, things that no one else can see but you. Much of what you find, you will discover that you have already known—intuitive perceptions about reality that you have known your entire life, but have lacked the ability to explain. You know that something is missing or that some-thing is wrong, but you've been unable to pinpoint it.

Yes, life goes on around you as normal, but often nothing seems normal about it. What is real and what is imagined? What is truth and what is lie? Instinct tells you there is something different out there, a different reality or a perspective on our existence that super-sedes the world itself, giving clarity to realities beyond the physical.

So I'm inviting you, even daring you, to look beyond what you currently see; to look inside as well as out. Perhaps God might reveal an entirely different view of the world—a view that does "not look at the outward appearances"[3] nor focuses on "the things which are seen."[4] I beckon you to peer "over the edge" of physical realities and gaze into the spiritual—a vast existence that permeates everything we can touch and see; a paradigm that gives clarity to the struggles we face; a new way of seeing that gives purpose and meaning to all we do, all we are, and all we will become.

Chapter 3

The Lie

Has any man ever obtained inner
harmony by simply reading about the
experiences of others? Not since the
world began has it ever happened.
Each man must go through the fire
himself. [1]

—Norman Douglas

E very human is born in a personal desert. Empty hearts search dry
and dusty lands for anything to fill the perpetual void in the soul
of a man separated from God. Into the emptiness of our souls
continual waves of worldly lies flood our minds. Within and beyond
this world, the devil prowls about as well, ready and willing to fulfill
desires (albeit temporarily) as long as it accomplishes two things:
distraction from worshiping God and derailing our created purposes.

Satan knows his most effective offense in the Western world
is a covert one. If he were to blatantly show his face (as he does in
many other parts of the world) those in Christian and post-Christian
communities would take up arms. Instead, he moves in stealth, behind
the scenes, subtly twisting and distorting; convincing others that he
really isn't a reality. With defenses dropped, he can roam freely,

guiding demise undetected rather than attempting a frontal assault. The assault will come in due time, but for now Satan appears to be content to remain hidden in the wings, allowing the world's media machine to deceive and desensitize as it moves everything away from what God intended.

The human soul is desperate. Working together in seamless harmony, the world and the devil appeal to the desires of the thirsty soul. In the midst of the heat, mirages appear just on the horizon—hopeful images of cool, wet satisfaction. Encouraging you to chase the mirage, however it manifests itself to you, they feed your desires while offering illusions of fulfillment. Satan tempts and baits for his solitary purpose of trying to deny God of what is rightly His. Those of the world lure you on, using you for the fulfillment of their own desires. Together they move in unison, seeking to influence our society as a whole… but in the end we find that we have been led in circles. Our desires yet unsatisfied, our feelings festering and blistered on the dry sands.

As residents of the information age, our homes are open conduits of an endless stream of images and ideas. Television, internet, radio… a constant flow of music and media fill the rooms of our lives. Image after image bombard us, presenting the illusion of something real, something of value, something of substance that can be found apart from God. Each time we give in we find brief but fleeting satisfaction—just enough to wet our appetites for more, but never enough to fill us in lasting measure. From the cradle to the grave, many of us have come to accept that this life is little more than a series of momentary satisfactions.

Let there be no doubt: from the beginning of time, the Father of Lies has tempted humanity incessantly and strategically, targeting the areas where our flesh and souls are most vulnerable. Both Satan and the world work from the dualistic worldview, the view that says the physical and spiritual realms are distinct and separate. When Satan tempted Christ, and when he and the world tempt us today, the temptations emerged from the lie that says inner spiritual peace for the soul comes from physical, outward circumstances: the things you can acquire or control, the total makeover that allows you to become someone else, the new job, the new house on the Boulevard, the new car in the garage, etc.

Once someone has been infused with this most basic of lies, they will be willing to buy into almost anything that the marketing world tries to sell. That is a fact. I know; I've worked for some of the largest corporations on the planet. I've spent plenty of time with marketing firms and public relations companies who are experts at appealing to desire and selling their wares. Like the old man behind the curtain in the Wizard of Oz, I've watched them pull the levers time and time again. From the products you buy to the movies you see… nearly every purchase takes place at the instigation of the media/marketing machine that appeals to our basic desires in a dualistic context.

With precision and expertise they aim at our felt emotional needs, arousing the senses, and instilling the "need" to fulfill them. Acceptance, fame, pleasure, fun, admiration, success… buy what they are selling and you buy into the illusion that they are offering what you want.

All the marketers need to do is to paint a picture of what they want you to want… with you just slightly outside of the frame, longing for what's on the inside. By drawing on the ancient temptations, they simply create a dream—a vision for life as you *desire* it to be, convincing you that it *can* be achieved, that it is in reach as long as you purchase their product. Never mind that it is all a mirage, founded on a faulty dualistic view of reality.

They will sell you anything they can, but they can't offer you the thing that you truly need, because it's never been in the inventory: peace. In fact, they wouldn't sell that to you even if they could. They know that the person who has found true meaning, purpose, and contentment is a lousy repeat customer.

What strategies do they use to exert their influence? First, they avoid human defenses. They simply go around the resistance that goes up when humans feel manipulated or coerced. Then they appeal to the senses; cohabitating with felt needs and dreams; disarming personal discernment… Finally, they turn up the intensity. When we become desensitized and unstimulated by current levels of input, the media machine creates images that are more graphic and products that are more intriguing. They also become more and more skilled at convincing us that what they offer is what we need for fulfillment and meaning in life. Significantly it is all then packaged and presented, but not as clear temptation or manipulation, but as *entertainment*.

THE DREAM MACHINE

Throughout the developed world, a mechanism of mammoth proportion persistently and pervasively churns away 24/7/365, creating a dream—a vision of desire promising inner fulfillment, peace, and power. The machine does its continual work unbeknownst to most, ignored by almost everyone else, and understood by only a few. It is so prevalent, so constant, that we have become numb to its presence. I've seen it in action, from corporate America to the sidewalks of my neighborhood in Beverly Hills. It's called the "Dream Machine."

Media is powerful, but the mediums themselves are clearly benign. Like a gun which can be used for either good or for evil, the products of the media machine stretch across the spectrum from light to dark. For thousands of years entertainment has offered a brief departure from reality. It gives the viewer a chance to momentarily depart from the daily grind or temporarily see life through the eyes of another or (as in the case of the Greek tragedy) to savor the darker sides of reality while not having to live it out. To this end, the entertainment has legitimate value.

Media can be a conduit of worship, education, and communication. It is used to connect, to relax, and to numb. It is also used to exploit and to pervert the most beautiful and sacred gifts of God. Who's to blame for the darker aspects? Everyone. In all honesty, the escalation could be stopped by either the industry or the consumers; meaning that responsibility lies with us all.

Biologists use a term called "mutual parasitism," which defines relationships in nature where two organisms suck what they want from the other to the benefit or satisfaction of both. (A special saltwater leech, for example, attaches itself to sharks, feasting on byproducts of the shark's scavenger lifestyle while at the same time cleansing the shark's skin of potentially dangerous bacteria.) Such it is in any economy, but it is particularly graphic in the media industry. Following an ever present video/audio Pied Piper, we allow ourselves to be led away by the Dream Machine. For dozens of hours a week we are happy to soak in the illusion—an escape, perhaps, from the otherwise dull and meaningless existence of our own personal desert.

You've heard the statistics. According to Steve Glen and Jane Nelsen, Ed.D., "Up to the age of eighteen, children spend an average of 18,000 hours watching television. During that time they see an average of 180,000 minutes of commercials which teach them that self-medication and instant gratification are desirable, that warmth and closeness are easily obtainable through using the right products or services, and that the greatest success our sports heroes and other celebrities can aspire to involves hustling beverages and products."[2]

Long before working in Hollywood, I recognized how the machine worked, describing it in my journals:

> Creativity is by far a greater gift than pure intelligence.
> For without it, all you are is someone else's idea…
> …The irony is, the mass media has tried to satisfy both ideologies…
> …Within the framework of pop culture, hedonism, narcissism, pre-pubonic sexual cataclysm, and advertising…
> …Which subjugates the weak to a singular thought process, "stay tuned for more input"…
> … Sad how complacency and ignorance walk together to comprise our socially correct moral character.

Money keeps the gears turning, of course. According to a World Advertising Trends 2007 report, advertisers in the U.S. spent $163,000,000,000 (that's one hundred and sixty-three billion!) dollars in 2006 marketing their products.[3] These are hard earned funds from companies that depend on programming that makes you "stay tuned for more input." A sobering perspective is to remember that these marketing dollars drive us consumers to buy trillions of dollars of goods and services.

SHOCK ME, PLEASE

Since money is the fuel for the Dream Machine, one thing dominates the media economy: ratings. Built on this fact is a corporate structure that reflects these fiscal realities. Like its political counterpoint in Washington, the media culture in LA and New York is fickle and brutal. One moment you're hot, the next you're not. One day you're in the center, the next day they don't even know you're gone.

The Dream Machine must captivate its audience and it has become an expert at it. The result is the entertainment equivalent of "shock and awe." The media elite are fully aware of the desire of human flesh for power, pleasure, and adventure. To fuel these hungers they continually push for more progressive, more intense experiences for the consumer. The things that were "cutting edge" yesterday are dull today. What is revolutionary today will be the norm tomorrow. In order to maintain market share, the new norm must then again be ramped up to maintain competitive ratings.

The progression is easy to see. It wasn't so long ago that television executives refused to show couples in the same bed, even if they were married. If you wanted to see anything below Elvis's waist while he was dancing, you'd have to go to the movie theaters (the swaying of his hips to the music was considered much too provocative to be viewed in the home). The degradation that has taken place has almost become cliché. By hundreds of small steps and hundreds of forks in the road, Hollywood has ended up hundreds of miles away from where it started.

Casualties on the side of the road include the inner character of the actors themselves. Many began their careers "pop-corn clean" but allowed themselves to be lured into compromise by the temptations of fame and fortune. Britney Spears, Jessica Simpson, Christina Aguilera… all were willingly pushed across the line by the demands of the machine and their own desperate thirst for fame. Striving to be relevant in an ever changing society, superstars like Madonna often become chameleons, doing *anything* to stay at the top of the headlines. They must continually "update their packaging" to keep up with consumer demand for change and newness.

It's the way the world's system works: illusions of hope poured into the dry and empty soul of humanity, forming an escalating cycle of desire and temporary fulfillment. It's self-perpetuating, driven by the winds of society and economics... and I see no end. We continue to cross moral lines that are monumental, accepting the ever-increasing entertainment shock and awe as a perpetual component of advancing culture. Willingly, we allow ourselves to be drawn into the intrigue of the dark side of our humanness.

REALITY CHECK

The most dangerous and insidious aspect of the mirage created by the Dream Machine is this: it appears so *real*. Constant exposure to vivid and emotional material contorts our worldview, particularly when it is absorbed by the mind without scrutiny (as entertainment usually is). To the thirsty, hopeful soul trying to find meaning and purpose in the desert, the mirage of the Dream Machine becomes mentally tangible, as if it can, in reality, give sustenance to our being. In actuality, however, there is nothing real about it.

On the screen, the dream is brought to life by actors; paid professionals who project an image that has little or nothing to do with who they really might be. Yet the audience uses these characters as points of reference for their own identities, making it unclear what is fact and what is fiction.

Setting the stage and writing the scripts are powerfully talented people—men and women with incredible creative skills. They concoct intriguing scenarios that appeal to the senses and the desires—painting with shadows of truth that resonate with the frequency of our desperate lives. Our emotions connect with what we see. The images touch the center of our longings strongly enough to keep us engaged. As the dream unfolds, we identify it as something necessary to our psyche. It rivets us, keeping us seated through one more commercial—advertisements which inform us of yet another thing we need to find happiness and meaning.

Because it is labeled "entertainment," it flows into our souls largely unchecked. We would never accept actors or script writers as legitimate educators and yet they undeniably mold our perceptions. Has anyone checked their resumes? Are these the philosophers seeking truth or the theologians trying to grasp the nature of God? No, they aren't even themselves. They are professionals, paid to portray someone else—usually a fictional character who doesn't even exist. ("Reality TV" is probably the ultimate oxymoron.)

Great danger emerges when the lines between the mirage and reality become distorted. The intensity, the numbing, and the level of saturation that we experience as members of the current media culture, is profound. It's not just entertainment anymore; it's not just a brief departure from life. We are so saturated with its presence that the very fabric of mainstream society is now *defined* by the media.

The Dream Machine is now so pervasive and so effective, that our minds no longer take the time to filter out what is virtual from what is actual. The heart, stirred by powerful emotion and desire, no longer discerns truth from lie. The machine changes our perceptions of current reality, and these perceptions will guide us into the future. From our music to our movies, and now with hundreds of channels of satellite and cable TV, we allow ourselves to be lured into a world that defines who we should be, how things should work, and what we must have to be successful and fulfilled.

Shock and sell, shock and sell… that's the pattern. So what if the shock doesn't satisfy? That's ideal for the marketer, ensuring a repeat audience for repeated sales. That's actually the goal. If the entertainment served only as a brief reprieve for those who actually do fold clothes and pick kids up from school, then a respectable end would have been reached. But what happens when the unreal world on the screen becomes a point of reference for the comparatively dull and repetitive nature of day-to-day living? What happens in the heart when the glamour and the passion and the power portrayed on the tube take root in the heart, arousing a hunger and a desire for things that exist only in the imagination?

On a certain level, it's amazing how the Dream Machine has integrated itself into modern life… with billions of people oblivious to its power over thought. Flowing continually into the mind, the Dream Machine shapes reality on an individual and social level. It now does the thinking for the unthinking masses.

Certain movies had a powerful affect on my thinking and I created my own realities from these illusionary media images. The movie *The Sure Thing* and the classic *Animal House* left me with a seductive portrayal of the college party scene. I intentionally crafted a lifestyle that paralleled these images during my fraternity years. What my friends and I saw on the screen became our daily experiences as we ran unbridled and without sense of consequence.

The movie *The Doors* resonated deep in my soul on an even more profound, philosophical level. The movie was released at the peak of my drug years and chronicled the life of Jim Morrison, the rock and roll icon of the 60's. What I saw in the movie meshed with all I was seeking in college as I explored new sensations and new visions of reality. His journey into mind expansion and his desire to see beyond the confines of the world resonated in my soul, validating my thinking at the time. I watched Morrison transcend the norm by escaping the confines of self-limitation. He stretched the barriers of traditional conceptualization—the lines of reality melded together according to his wishes. Dark and self-destructive, I perceived that Morrison was nonetheless a genius and he became my role model for existential exploration. His realities expanded beyond the capacity of mortal minds; he found truth in a universe of his own making—and he affirmed all I was pursuing, all that I was trying to embrace. I even felt a tangible connection with the actor who brought Morrison to life on the screen. Val Kilmer's movements, his words, his voice, his message—it was brilliant acting, further immortalizing Jim Morrison and all he stood for. Val drew me into himself with something dark and real, something noble and enticing… In my mind, Kilmer personified Jim Morrison, and I wanted to personify both of them. They became dark heroes, my mentors, and I continued to conform my reality to theirs.

The Dream Machine has created a mirage in the desert of the human soul; the images the entertainment industry project are false visions of what life *can* be like and *should* be like. Indiscriminating individuals embrace the dream as something that *is* reality. As the masses identify the dream as a *potential* reality, the machine molds and shapes what *will* be. Fiction becomes self-fulfilling—yet because it is based on the lie of a dualistic worldview, it fills nothing.

Think about it. Think, think, please. Modern media is intended to manipulate your senses and appeal to your deepest desires, even as it dulls your mind. In the name of entertainment, it circumvents logic, avoiding mental scrutiny as it stimulates an emotional response. It is also highly effective in its affect and persuasion. Philosopher Arthur Schopenhauer states it this way:

> No one ever convinced anybody by logic; and even logicians use logic only as a source of income. To convince a man, you must appeal to his self-interest, his desires, his will.[4]

Ratings are designed to protect the mind of a child, but to what advantage is adult discernment? Perhaps we have a slightly more refined filter for sifting out what is real and what is not. Perhaps we have slightly better definitions of what is right and what is wrong than the child. But aren't our desires and longings more refined as well? Aren't we equally (if not more) vulnerable to insinuation and the images that affirm our lusts? Don't we allow our minds to be led into more mature versions of fantasy and discontent?

And to what advantage is the Christian? Our bodies and minds continually interface with the world. In what proportion are we exposed to lies as opposed to truth? Realistically, aren't we probably getting at least 90 percent of our input from the lies of the Dream Machine and maybe 10 percent from truth affirming sources? Be honest. *Think about it.*

The devil is smart. Assume that he has an IQ of about six billion. If he can take your soul he will. If he can't, he will divert your attention away from God. If he can't divert your attention, he will wait for an opening and use it to your destruction. Likewise, the Dream Machine is highly efficient in shaping the habits and desires of individuals and society. In the din of constant noise and input, defenses drop. We allow the unthinkable to flow into our homes in the name of entertainment, things that we would never, ever allow on our streets. Yet without the energy to discern or divide lie from truth, these things find their way into our souls—and from the soul emerges a dual life.

By separating the physical from the spiritual, most Christians have assimilated a contorted hybrid worldview... and our outward lives reflect it. To a great extent we live in congruence with the rules of the world. Compartmentalized in another corner of our existence is God, His still small voice often drowned out by the sheer magnitude of the messages we get from other sources. We have conformed to worldly values and pursuits in an attempt to find meaning and peace. One moment we strive to find it in comfort, possessions, power, and pleasure. For an hour or two a week we attempt to find it in worship. We have even come to judge worship as if it's entertainment—exciting, emotional, boring, fun. Haven't we really just taken the secular worldview of success and dressed it up in Christian clothing? If we misunderstand the basic nature of our existence, the essential nature of our battles, then *everything* becomes susceptible to the lure of the mirage, even things pertaining to worship, to fellowship, to Truth.

All search for peace and love, but if we buy into the lie, it is actually *impossible* to experience authentic peace and love. Only after seeing what the world really is, only after understanding the Truth, can we find peace... for that peace comes only from true intimacy with God in which the physical and the spiritual know no boundaries. Can one come to truly believe in such an existence outside of experience? The existentialist would say "no," and I'm inclined to agree. The sobering truth is that the vast majority of us come to Truth unwillingly, not of our own volition. The transformation of a worldview is usually forced on us—the result of a brutal shattering of the dreams we have created, the dissolution of the mirage we have been pursuing.

Meaning cannot be found in the illusion of dreams of human creation. Still, the desire for both peace and meaning drives us. That's what you are looking for. I know, because I have looked for the same thing. I searched long and hard, but what I found was not so much a thing as it was an answer to the questions I didn't even know I was asking.

In the life of every individual, the time must come when the dream is revealed for what it is not. Each must wake up to the foundational errors in our personal views of the world. Each must choose a course that recognizes the lie and begin a journey where the spiritual and the physical are seen as seamlessly integrated. Our prayer, perhaps, should not be, "If I should die before I wake…" Rather we should wonder what life would be "If I should wake before I die…"

In the end, we must all stand in our own private desert and face the lies behind the temptations that bombard us. That's where it begins, in the desert. From there, the road to Truth is very much a journey, a journey that each must travel alone.

Chapter 4

A Journey Universal

We shall not cease from exploration
and the end of all our exploring will be
to arrive where we started and know
the place for the first time.[1]

— T. S. Eliot

Hear the conductor's impetuous cry,
"All destinations unknown! Please
board as your life is called."

—Personal journal entry

It is often said that "life is a journey"—a traveling through time from one destination to another. Fraught with detours and difficulties, mountaintops and valleys, the journey lacks nothing in the way of tears and laughter as we seek purpose and fulfillment. For some it's an amiable journey, wandering through the years of life driven by the winds of the lie. Others push on into a cloud of anger. They know there must be something more, but are frustrated in their inability to find that "something" that will satisfy their desires for meaning and peace. Some fall into despondency, aware of being lost in the desert, but without the illumination or the inspiration to do anything about it.

Still, there are others who protect the lie at all costs—even violently so—guarding it as the only hope they have for making sense of life in the sand.

Then there are those who recognize both the lie *and* the need for Truth. For them life becomes a quest—a quest to find answers of substance to the questions that haunt us. These are willing to forgo the assumptions of the world and seek fresh perspectives in order to discover the purpose of their existence. They know that a route out of the lies *must* be discerned; for the very essence of life depends upon it. Frederick Buechner said, "My assumption is that the story of any one of us is in some measure the story of us all."[2] Such is the quest for personal Truth; it is a universal journey that is required of all who truly seek peace and meaning.

The prelude to my journey begins at the dawn of my memories, somewhere around age five, where those earliest of memories are filled with the things of God. I had come to Him as a child in every way: simple, wide-eyed, and full of confident naivety. I didn't question, I just believed. In the simplicity of preadolescence, this virgin faith grew in unadulterated innocence. It wasn't deep, but it was comfortable, a simple expression of who I thought I was. By fifth grade I had read the Bible cover to cover. Sometimes it seemed God spoke to me directly, words coming inaudibly yet clearly. While walking home from school in sixth grade the words "Philippians 4:9" popped into my head. I had no clue what this Bible verse said, but I saw the reference as if it were written in my head. At home I looked up the passage:

> Whatever you have learned or received or heard from me, or seen in me—put it into practice. And the God of peace will be with you.

I adopted the verse as my life-purpose statement. What I heard I practiced and God's peace was with my soul. In seventh grade I felt called to be a missionary to Africa. Socially, my faith was coddled in the relative protection of a Christian junior high where I grew in sheltered insulation. Belief was genuine and it was natural; nothing contrived or preconceived. I was just being me.

Slowly, the seasons began to change. On a weekend youth group retreat in my eighth grade year, I explored Joshua Tree for the first time. In the stark, barren landscape, I walked with my friends and with God. We saw Him simply and clearly, even in this place of desolation… but there were changes. We were no longer children—though we had a long way to go before becoming adults. That weekend we drifted through the jumble of stones at our leisure, impervious to the dangers around us and within us. It was "fun" and it was the last "event" of my adolescent Christianity; the summation of youthful spirituality.

When I was sixteen, my family moved from California to Ohio. In California I was just a regular kid. I was a good student who played football, soccer, and baseball and I had a group of friends that accepted me for who I was as a Christian. When I arrived in Ohio, I soon realized I was very different from the others. The music I listened to, the clothes I wore, the things I liked to do… *everything* that I had been in California was out of place in my new high school. My choice to not drink further isolated me from my peers. I played soccer and found some friends but I couldn't find my niche in the crowd. Day after day I walked the halls in silence; the phone rarely rang on the weekends. I longed for the acceptance of my peers. I became angry that I did not fit in with the world and grew tired of playing the good boy.

In frustration, I eventually made the decision to drink—a decision that would define who I would be and what I would strive for over the next two decades. Along with the choice to party I also changed my attitude. While never consciously deciding to leave my childhood faith, I now used all of my God-given talents to glorify myself instead of Him. A competitive and obsessive nature took over; before long I was one of the biggest drinkers in my school. With my new attitude and desire to party, I quickly gained the friends I was searching for. This further fueled my passion to party and to be the center of attention. I had given up God to be successful in the world.

I had chosen the lie of the Dream Machine, and Satan was more than willing to accommodate me.

By the time I went to college, every spare ounce of energy was put into "fun at all costs" and it worked. I had become the consummate "fraternity boy" and achieved tremendous success (at least as success was defined in that subculture). I had a huge group of great friends, played soccer for my college, and partied almost every night. My pride drove me on a daily basis. I thought I had it all but I was really just blind, selfish, egotistical, stuck-up, judgmental, and shallow.

For a while I felt lingering remorse and I sought a shadow of repentance for my lifestyle, but the frequency and intensity of sin began to dull my conscience. Where my childhood had been lived in contrast to the things of the world, I entered adulthood completely immersed in the dream of the machine. I was glad that I had not succumbed to the religious boundaries of the typical Christian who had insulated themselves in naivety. In growing arrogance and pride I judged them for their intolerance and pitied them for the limits with which they had shackled themselves. Certain songs, such as *Losing My Religion* by R.E.M. became anthems for my new life.

A veil of self-deceit and self-conceit descended. I lost the gift of discernment and replaced it with TV, movies, and music; these things became my moral compass, indicating where I needed to go to be fulfilled. It was all about me. It was all about fun. I felt invigorated, affirmed, and empowered. I wasn't on a path to *destroy* my life; I was convinced that I had *found* life and was living as I was created to live. A new paradigm for right and wrong replaced the conviction of the Spirit of God. As a result, I quit asking for forgiveness. There was no need to repent if indeed I was "living right." The definitions and implications of sin (and therefore the need to repent) were conveniently stuffed into the religious compartment of my life and held there under the illusion of dualism, allowing my mind to condone and pursue blatant hedonism. The plot had thickened. The lie had intervened between my innate desire for intimacy with God and the love that He is willing to give. I had become a poster child for Romans 1:25:

For they exchanged the truth of God for a lie, and worshiped and served the creature rather than the Creator.

In my heart, as in every heart, the lie manifested itself uniquely. For some the lie tempts with comfort or security or wealth. For others the lure of acceptance and adventure draws one into the illusion. Regardless of the specifics, the core of the lie is always the same, telling us that true meaning and fulfillment can be found in the physical realm.

To the extent that we buy into the lie we will pursue acceptance, adventure, possessions, power, knowledge, or accomplishment in manmade things, rather than in God. Those who perceive that the dream is out of their reach will feel resigned to a defensive life of rejection, conflict avoidance, protection, or depression. Consider this carefully: isn't your mind immediately catapulted in one of these two directions (desperate pursuit or hopeless resignation) the moment you look toward anything but God for peace and meaning in your soul?

I clearly took the aggressive route. Hook, line, and sinker I swallowed the bait of Satan. With increasing intensity I succumbed to temptation and I did so in willful calculation with my body and my mind. Increasingly, drugs were having an influence on the flow of thoughts in my mind. They allowed me to see the world differently, skewing the boundaries of reality, changing perceptions about what was and what might be. I questioned everything: life, death, ethics, morals… and I found answers in drug-induced ponderings. What my mind perceived at the moment determined what was true.

Through it all, however, God never left me or my deeper thoughts. While looking in all the wrong places I was really searching for what only God can supply and He graciously gave me reminders of Truth. While partying on spring break in Mexico, a friend dared me to write about what I was experiencing. In my current state of mind, I just wrote, not remembering one line of text from another. But when I finished, I was shocked to see what I had penned:

To ponder God's creations,
Is to ponder the essence of our being,
To see into the light,
The breath that saves us all.
It's not to ask but to believe.
To see is to be an unbeliever.

It was the first poem I ever wrote and through it I realized that despite my sin and regardless of how far I had allowed my emotions to drift away from God, my soul still yearned for Him. It was a sobering thought.

THE BEST OF BOTH WORLDS

Outwardly, life seemed to be going great. I was experiencing the best that the world had to offer. None of it was intentionally evil or malicious; I was just the fraternity guy gone wild. I had friends, women, and (due to countless hours spent in the weight room) a powerful body. As a sophomore I won the "Greek Physique" contest, and I had the ego to match. My entire self-worth was entwined with such things. I had become part of the world; I had become the lie.

From time to time I'd retreat in an introspective mood where I'd write poetry and ponder life and God... then I'd walk away from it and jump back into the party. My pursuits were about 97 percent fun and 3 percent faith. I had a completely fragmented life, dividing into components what God intended to be whole.

Through fairly complicated mental gymnastics and self-convincing pep talks, I was able to temporarily avoid what psychologists call "cognitive dissonance"—a mental disharmony that occurs when the mind tries to accept two conflicting concepts. By carefully selected logic I twisted clear scriptural realities, contorting my perception of God to fit my own preferences. My beliefs became eclectic; a strange mixture of the Bible and philosophy as I reached out to thinkers who affirmed my evolving worldview.

Spinoza intrigued me as he defined God in geometric terms. I admired the sacrifices he made; forsaking the material world, living in poverty to avoid polluting his consciousness with physical concerns. I resonated with the thoughts and choices of Voltaire. He held a defiant and rebellious stance against organized religion and it's graphic failures, while simultaneously holding to faith even while he gorged his fleshly appetites. At the time, I shared his thoughts as I shunned religious gatherings. "Church" was getting high and listening to Pink Floyd. My "worship" took place in the cathedrals of philosophy. "Holy days" involved trips that raised my senses and indulgences to higher levels. During my senior year of college I went to Hollywood with a friend where we submerged ourselves in the Sunset Boulevard club scene. It was the peak of LA nightlife, the pinnacle of my pursuits, and a complete immersion into a world that sought pleasure without restraint. I loved it. Night after night we lived my dream, experiencing everything that I thought life should be.

I was the epitome of the double-minded man, "… like the surf of the sea, driven and tossed by the wind."[3] Confident of God's forgiveness on a spiritual level, I ran free in the physical. I had never really considered the worldview behind my thoughts, but I was certain that my relationship with Him could be compartmentalized, left in its corner without consequence as I pursued earthly pleasure.

I was an extreme specimen in the museum of dualism and I didn't even know it. Others feel the tension as they try to find a comfortable balance between fleshly desires and our inner spiritual yearnings. Some people appear to sustain a peaceful balance indefinitely to the end. Others are torn by cognitive dissonance on a daily basis. Either existence is a tragedy. Neither leads to life as God designed it to be lived: *over the edge*, with physical and spiritual realities inseparably integrated.

A CRACK IN THE FAÇADE

My first inclination that something was truly wrong with my dual life came in the form of a dream during my senior year of college. I called it "a dream within a dream." Throughout the entire night, my consciousness vacillated between sleep and wakefulness. I would sleep and dream vivid images, then I would wake every half hour or so and ponder what I had seen. When I'd sleep again, the dream would continue from where it left off, the vision continually unfolding:

I was suspended in space. Planets were drifting towards me, passing by on my right—hundreds of them, one after the other—images of God's creation. The last planet stopped in front of me, rotating before my eyes. I then found myself upon it, standing on a flat plain, looking at buildings in the distance. It was a city, an image of the things created by man. The city was normal in color and all appeared as it should; tall buildings, clean streets, beautiful trees... full of life and vibrancy. As I watched, it was as if a veil lifted before my eyes; everything turned to a neutral sand color—washed out tans void of hue. Inside the city I found no life; the buildings vacant, the streets silent and dead. Then it was as if entropy was accelerated. The city decayed before my eyes, as if the life-giving moisture had been drained from it. I reached out and the buildings turned to dust in my hand.

To this day the dream is still so clear. I can recall it verbatim, as if I had physically experienced it. The meaning behind what I had seen was clear. Following God's birthing of the planets and earth, humanity built its own reality. From a brief distance it all seemed so significant, so permanent—the impressive result of man's engineering glory and a symbol of progress and achievement. But up close the city's lifelessness was revealed. In and of itself, it was vacant, dead, and barren. It was *life without God*—which is no life at all—and destined to crumble. Physical reality was like sand... and it was slipping through my fingers.

As graphic as the vision was, it should have come as no surprise. The basic laws of physics and even a superficial skimming of history clearly attest to the temporary nature of the physical world and the future of our godless pursuits. The timeless wisdom of Solomon repeatedly warns of this impending reality in passages such as Ecclesiastes:

> I wanted to see what was worthwhile for men to do under heaven for the few days of their lives. I undertook great projects: I built houses for myself and planted vineyards... I also owned more herds and flocks than anyone in Jerusalem before me. I amassed

silver and gold for myself and the treasure of kings and provinces... Yet when I surveyed all that my hands had done and what I had toiled to achieve, everything was meaningless, a chasing after the wind.[4]

It shouldn't have taken a dream to see this. But like most, my self-imposed ignorance of this fact had allowed me to avoid the obvious: *this world and all that is in it will not last and is ultimately meaningless.* In the weeks following the dream I began to see things a little bit more clearly. As I did, anxiety crept into my heart. I felt a gap narrowing, closing the distance between the dream I had been living and the nightmare I was creating for myself. I was beginning to reap what I was sowing. After six years of the lie, my soul had been degraded in every way and I had nothing of value to show for it.

One morning I was lying in the bath tub, trying to come down from the night before. Chemicals swirled in my brain as my mind tried to connect my thoughts. Nothing seemed to make sense except for two things: I was alone in this world... and I was scared.

I started to try to rebalance things—a little more God, a little less of everything else. I started to detach myself from the life I had led. I backed out of the fraternity and cut back on drugs and alcohol. I was heading in a different direction, but rather than making life better, these adjustments only caused conflict. The acceptance of my peers waned. All the "fun" was beginning to dissolve. In its place an intense mental persecution and fear descended on my heart.

God was graciously revealing Truth. The game I had been playing was clearly no game at all. This was a war, a war for the soul; and when I started to resist, pleasures were no longer lavished on me for my waywardness. As I started to see into the unseen, the evil one stepped over the edge and showed his face. One evening, alone on my bed, I felt a chill go over my body. It was as if a disconcerting and unwelcome breeze had filtered in from outside. There in the upper corner of the room a massless, faceless, silhouette of black hovered in silence. I prayed against the spirit in the name of Jesus. The form casually dissipated, leaving me alone trying to catch my breath. I sat stunned and startled to have found myself in such a place. It was the first indication that the world and the deceiver were real; the first revelation that they were, indeed, my enemies.

CIVILIZED

Shortly after graduation, I married Tiffany who I had met the summer before my senior year. Beautiful in both spirit and appearance, God used her as a stabilizing influence in my heart. Marriage and children changed the outward contour of my days, adding a new, richer dimension to everything I was. A deep appreciation of my wife and heartfelt fatherly devotion took the place of many things. I was becoming socialized, conformed to more acceptable behavior in the eyes of society and religion, and the years began to slip by.

But I was still in hot pursuit of the things of the world and I defined myself by my job, my sports, and my travels. I was still addicted to the "high" and found it in adrenaline laced sports. I indulged my passions with motorcycle racing that took me to 150 miles per hour. I pushed myself to succeed in every situation, measuring my self-worth by my worldly accomplishments. I couldn't see it at the time, but I was always trying to prove something to someone or earn acceptance through what I did. (It wasn't much more than an adult version of the high school drinking scene.) There was momentary substance to it, but it never satisfied, proving to be shallow and empty.

In the eyes of the mainstream, I may have been "towing the line" a little better, but the line was full of tension. I was a "success," but I began to experience a growing void as the things of the world lost their edge and their taste. In the privacy of my journal, I was honest with what I faced:

Self criticism—criticism of how I have come to view life and the emptiness I feel striving after the suburban dream. I fear it's a never ending dream that will end with me being cold and lost. This is what I must strive to avoid. I need to rediscover the love of "life," the life not seen by most, the path of reasoning. To take vacations and wander through the desert. To see the magic of a sunset. To stop and soak in life. For life is all encompassing. It surrounds us, penetrates us with its Gift. To see God in the blossoms of a tree… I have sacrificed this perception to achieve the wonderful family and career I have. Now I must strive to grab hold of the perception I lost and rediscover life as a man. For life is fleeting, but our souls are eternal.

Like countless others, I had been caught in the lukewarm middle—neither hot nor cold, neither wounded nor healed, neither useful nor destructive. As I lingered in this half-Christian, half-worldly state, the devil left me alone. And why wouldn't he? Was I a threat? Was I a challenge? No, I was part of his team. I was just another gear in the Dream Machine, a Christianized version of Satan's exact intent. Pink Floyd described me perfectly in their song *Comfortably Numb*. I was neutralized and ineffectual for anything that mattered… and deep down, I knew it.

I was facing the great tragedy that many realize at life's end—not the inevitability of death, but the fact that so few who die have ever really *lived.* I was drifting in the flow of the culture and it was going nowhere:

I am weary. The journey is long but my path is uncertain. My heart and mind are at war. Shall I be rational or emotional? Shall I live for me or for others? My Lord, time has taken its toll. The emotions have faded like sand in an hourglass. Where does it end? How does it change? What is the catalyst to erase the hurt, the apathy, the memories, and begin a new life? Is it possible?

Answer this question and I'll no longer walk on the razor's edge. Leave this question hanging, and I shall drift aimlessly like an actor reading his lines, following the script of another.

Help me to find my way home once again, Lord, for I
have lost my way.

THE DECISION

Perhaps it was instinct; perhaps it was an inner desperation
that intuitively drew me back to the mountains just before my thirty
second birthday. For the better part of a decade, our little family had
been moving around the globe following my work. Memphis, Cincinnati, London, Cincinnati again… now we were in Seattle. I had been
going back to church and the men's group was planning a weekend
winter retreat in the Cascade Mountains. It would be the first such
sojourn since the junior high school retreat to Joshua Tree nearly
twenty years prior.

The retreat itself was unremarkable and perhaps that's what
made it feel so outstanding. When I first came in to the meeting room,
it was filled with men—normal men, unpretentious in simple
surroundings. I stood in back as they worshiped and prayed. No band,
no flowery religious talk, no emotional hype… just men, just God,
just communicating with each other. It shook me from inside, waking
me from what seemed to be a long, long sleep. I had explored
meaning in the universe through mind alteration; I had tried to create
my own world in business; I had expounded on the nature of God in
the ethereal depths of philosophy… and I had missed it. I had lost
"the simplicity and purity of devotion to Christ." [5]

In the solitude of that retreat—alone in the crisp, cool, and
quiet breezes, standing with these normal men—I remembered that
which I had forgotten, that God is real and present in this crazy
world... that He was present in *me*. Among the trees and the rocks I
saw shadows of belief, *real* belief. I heard echoes of a distant faith, the
faith of a child who had once heard and seen so clearly. My heart was
returning Home. The wandering soul had come full circle and was
rediscovering peaceful intimacy with the Creator.

The impact of the realization was immediate and I left the
mountains with a new sense of resolve—with the sense that the
missing piece was being recovered. Back at home, however, reentry
was not the emotional utopia I had expected. Instead, I found myself

mentally tortured with irrational fears and uninvited feelings of anxiety. For a while I thought I might be going crazy, but Tiffany was being attacked the same way. Together we prayed and the plague of fears was lifted.

It was another lesson in the ways of the greater war. By restoring my allegiance to God, I had inadvertently made myself a target for evil. With no spiritual Geneva Convention to ensure that the enemy would fight fair, Satan had attacked unprovoked. Through prayer God had delivered and we were grateful. We knew that we had passed through an important junction. But we were tired from that battle and looking forward to a break from the warfare.

One week later we were on our way to the deserts of Southern California... and to Joshua Tree. The journey was just about to begin.

Chapter 5

The World Collapses

There is a God shaped vacuum in the
heart of every man which cannot be filled
by any created thing, but only by God,
the Creator, made known through Jesus.[1]
— Pascal

Any true journey begins with a realization, a moment of epiphany
that reveals the absolute necessity of one of two things: either
something *is* that must not be or something *is not* that must be. As
such, a *journey* is distinctly different from *wandering and drifting*
aimlessly in the current of society. No, the one who journeys does so
with purpose, intending to either escape or to embrace essential
elements that influence the very essence of life.

Humans, by nature, are creatures of comfort. Without a realization of the need for change we are inclined to remain as we are,
where we are, and who we are. To uproot our souls and move beyond
the status quo requires certain forces, forces that upset our sense of
comfort and complacency and propel us into the now necessary
unknown. The journey out of the desert of the lie begins with a
forceful awakening from the dream of the machine. Since one is not
even aware that he has been asleep, the realization itself is upsetting.

From birth we have been continually indoctrinated with the lie, the lie that says our value comes from what we have, what we do, and what we look like. It is all we have ever known. It is the unwritten, unspoken platform upon which our culture is built. By default, the lie leads us into repeated and fruitless endeavors as we errantly attempt to find in the physical world that which can only be embraced in the spiritual.

The awakening can come in many forms, but always follows one of two patterns. First, the lie is exposed through pain and unfulfilled desires; or second, it can be revealed by the haunting emptiness of success. Though diametrically different in appearance, both achieve the same result: the beginning of a journey that points one in the direction of God.

HARSH REALITIES

Joshua Tree should have changed my entire life. You would think that being the recipient of a modern day miracle would have changed my course. Remarkably, it did not. My interpretation of the event actually fed lies which were deeply entrenched in my psyche. I had always led a charmed life, the things of the world coming easily and excessively. After the fall it still looked like I could have it all, and *more.* I now felt certain that God's job was to save me and to empower me. I had looked death in the face and walked away victorious. God had proven to be faithful and dependable. I now saw Him as the ultimate right-hand man, a bodyguard to aid me in my pursuits.

While God had protected me from the final impact of the fall, I was still recovering from a concussion I received when I glanced off the side of the cliff on the way down. It hurt my head to go outside in the sun. I couldn't read more than a few lines in a book before I would get tired. For two weeks I stayed at home trying to get the strength to return to work. When I finally went back to work, it took great effort to function. I was a shell of my former self but I was quickly healing. I could feel myself getting stronger every day. As usual, I focused all my attention on myself, thinking that through my actions I would be restored and return to life as normal.

So I jumped back into life and that life was still all about me. Tiffany was astounded, stunned that I was resilient to change after such an event. She had been praying for a change in my life for years. A miracle had taken place, but it appeared to pass through my soul without consequence. I was stubborn beyond reason and I lacked humility. Though I had come to see the truth about physical and spiritual realities, the lie was still alive and well in my soul. God had taught me a lot through the fall in Joshua Tree, but my heart had failed the test.

A relatively minor car accident would prove to be my undoing. Five weeks after the fall, during my routine commute home from work, I was hit from behind by a youth pastor at a stop light, snapping my head back into the headrest. The impact compounded the concussion I had received from the fall in Joshua Tree, causing additional injury to my fragile head.

With one stone, Satan had wounded two birds. The crash would financially derail the youth pastor's plans to go overseas in mission work. And in a brief instant, all I held dear crumbled into a confused mess in the driver's seat. I drove home shaken and in shock, fearful of how my brain would react to the new trauma. I got my answer the next morning. All the symptoms from the previous concussion returned, now compounded by a multitude of new issues.

Now, every moment of the day I felt like I was on a ship out at sea during a storm, like I was drunk and unable to balance. The world was constantly moving even when I stood still. I couldn't carry more than five pounds or the pressure in my head would become unbearable. Minimal exertion—such as walking up a slight hill— would cause the pressure in my head to rise incredibly. I couldn't tilt my head up to look at the sky, or down to look at the ground, without feeling a tremendous shift in my skull that would make me feel like falling down. Peripheral vision was blurry and my balance and vision only got worse at night. My brain could only process so much information; once it was full, it had to shut down or I would feel claustrophobic in my own head. I wanted to run away from my own mind, but there was no escape from the pressure. The house had to be museum quiet or the sounds would drive me crazy. At work at Microsoft, I had an incredibly difficult time reading e-mail, let alone interpreting complex spreadsheets. With my body devoting all resources to restore my brain, I was an easy target for other physical illnesses. I contracted "walking pneumonia," draining what remained of my strength and stamina. This was followed by allergies, migraine headaches, and the strain of asthmatic breathing.

My life had been all about controlling my environment. But now I was no longer in control of anything, and fear rushed in to take the place of my vanishing self-confidence. One day I collapsed in tears on my stairs, crying as Tiffany tried to comfort me. As the tears fell, my fears and frustration welled. In ten weeks, I had gone from having it all to being reduced to nothing. Over the decades, I'd been blessed and protected; I had beaten the odds on so many things. Now it was blow after blow and I felt persecuted by God, who had always given me what I wanted. I was angry, extremely angry. And I was most angry at God. I screamed, "Why, God!?" The world and my thoughts imploded upon themselves. I was no longer a man; I was nothing. Everything that defined me as a person was ripped away without my consent. Nothing had clarity except my fears, and then these fears multiplied upon themselves. I feared that my fears would consume me, that I might disappear into my own tormented world. I couldn't understand why God saved me from certain death to then just allow me to be destroyed by a youth pastor. I couldn't see it then, but I understand now.

The incident had finally exposed my personal version of the lie; a lie I didn't even know I was living. I had sought satisfaction and peace for my soul in the physical world. Now, I was living out the vision I had seen: I had built a city unto myself and it had turned to sand. But this time, it wasn't a vision. It was *my* life slipping through my fingers… and I could feel it.

Everything I had, everything I thought I was, was being revealed as part of the mirage… and I was terrified. Fear flooded into every corner of my being as I realized that my sense of control had been nothing more than an illusion. I was afraid to take the steps from my car to my house. A brief walk down the sidewalk with my daughter, Audrey, induced panic attacks. It was fear like I had never known before. It wasn't a response to a clear outward threat; it radiated throughout my body and my mind from somewhere deep in my heart. God was stripping me of the lie and preparing me for a different kind of life.

PROMISE IN PAIN

"Pain," is such a relevant term. We block out its memory and adjust our lives to avoid it. It's one emotion in the realm of feelings, yet it overshadows most others. Pain can invade the body—or worse yet, the heart—exposing our most vulnerable places. Love, for example is the most desired of feelings, yet pain is its unfortunate by-product. (It's ironic that something that yields so much joy can cause so much sorrow if the desire for it is denied.)

Tim Hansel described it this way:

Pain. We all know what it tastes like. Whether its source is physical, emotional, mental or spiritual, its interruption in our lives disrupts and reshapes. It intercepts our hopes and plans; it rearranges our dreams. It always leaves a mark.[2]

In pain there is no future. Prior to the accident, I had always looked to the future with expectation. I was always ready to move upward and onward. With pain in the future, I found myself yearning for the past, wishing for the smaller things that used to make up my complaints. After six months of mental and physical struggle, my courage and patience were spent and I realized that death is not an unreasonable option. It is reasonable to wish the pain would subside by any means.

> You purchase pain with all that joy can give and die of nothing but a rage to live.[3]
> —Alexander Pope

Physically, I know I didn't have it as bad as many, many others. There are multitudes that would have gladly traded my struggles for their own. The majority of my pain and agony, however, came from my soul. I thought I was Superman, but the physical struggles I faced proved to be my Kryptonite. I was, after all, a mere mortal. I was vulnerable. I was weak. Every person has their own version of Kryptonite. Lurking in the bushes are threats to the things that we place on the throne of our lives, elements of the lie in which we have placed our trust, things that displace God from His rightful presence in our hearts. God was using my particular struggles to reveal the core of my desires and the lies that had displaced His Truth in my heart.

The lie says we are defined by what we do, what we have, and what we look like. God uses pain strategically and purposefully, revealing the fragile earthly things we rely on for false purpose and peace. Sometimes—probably *most* of the time—pain is the only thing that communicates through our thick skulls. (I had been in a miracle and I *still* didn't get the message.) Looking back I can see that the message from the accident was a divine gift; and that pain and fear were its wrapping. I had to be broken. I had to be cleansed and purged of my former self in order to be built back up as God intended me to be. Through pain and with pain He often strips us down to the point where we are like Moses, crushed—and finally ready to surrender to Truth. Like the shackles of a slave, the lie must be broken if we are to be truly free. Freedom often comes through the violent beating of the hammer on an anvil, until the man can walk uninhibited as intended, to the glory of an emancipating Master.

For the sake of our peace and our intimacy with Him, God knows that the lie cannot remain. With the love and firm grasp of a perfect Father, He uses both the fear and the pain to wake us up from false dreams in order to implant our hopes in things that are real and true.

> Those whom I love, I rebuke and I
> discipline. So be earnest, and repent.
> —Revelation 3:19

HOLLOW VICTORIES

Pain can find its way into the soul through unusual avenues, routes that one might never expect. Consider these thoughts from Arthur Schopenhauer:

Every epic and dramatic poem can only represent a struggle, an effort, a fight for happiness; never enduring and complete happiness itself. It conducts its heroes through a thousand dangers and difficulties to the goal; as soon as this is reached it hastens to let the curtain fall; for now there would remain nothing for it to do but to show that the glittering goal in which the hero expected to find happiness had only disappointed him, and that after its attainment he was no better off than before.[4]

"Success," as it is defined by the lies of the Dream Machine, comes with a haunting realization: accomplishment and attainment can lead to an emptiness beyond compare. Success, as well as pain, reveals the incapacity of worldly things to satisfy the soul in any lasting measure.

It seems so obvious, does it not, the pointless pursuit of power and greed? Those who desire money will never have enough; those whose god is power will forever be its servant; greed and ambition only result in loneliness and unfulfilled dreams. And in the end, we shall all die. The earth remains, just the players are exchanged. We do not remember those who came before us just as our descendents will forget those who came before them.

This truth is so contrary to the assumptions of the lie, that the human heart can barely comprehend it. Instead, we suppress it or ignore it. When perceptions of reality, viewed in honest reflection, reveal only further longing in the soul, is it any wonder that we should seek to numb the mind? Advertising, news, entertainment media... all contribute to the general decomposition of our imagination, dulling our senses. It is little wonder that suppression of the mind is quite legal in every society. Alcohol is a basic form of Western suppression and every culture finds something artificial to diffuse the vacancy found within the soul.

To climb to the top and find nothing there, having neither enjoyed the journey nor found substance at its end... does this not reveal that few have truly answered the question, "What is the meaning of life?" But where is one to go when the pinnacle of success is found to be void of peace and meaning? Does one face the mirage for what it is? Does one ignore the obvious and pick another desire to pursue? Having experienced the hollowness of the lie—and having no other alternative worldview—aren't we destined for anger, denial, suppression, or depression?

A STRANGE HOPE

I had discovered philosophy in college. In the writings of the great thinkers I found men who were courageous enough to venture beyond conventional wisdom and trite religious cliché in order to probe the depths of our existence with brutally honest questions. I loved the philosopher; I still do. Unfortunately, very few of them offered any tangible answers to the questions they so profoundly articulated.

> A philosopher is a blind man in a dark room looking for a black cat that isn't there. A theologian is the man who finds it. –H. L. Mencken[5]

The philosopher knows that the issues of pain and success are fundamental to life. But foundational to these issues is the issue of life itself. What is life? Look around and you see yourself among the masses, laboring and striving to achieve earthy goals—yet never fully understanding the reasons behind our desires. Is it too much to ask, *"Why?"* Who looks beyond our desires and asks the eternal question, *"Why?"* Nietzsche, Confucius, Siddhartha Gautama… all asked this question. They explored the humility of the soul and discovered the emptiness in this world. Few philosophers, however, are willing to take the next step and embrace a fulfillment that comes from beyond this world.

God told the prophet Jeremiah that He had a plan, a plan to "give you a future and a hope."[6] The hope He offered had little to do with physical circumstance, but rather finding true peace and meaning in the midst of any circumstance. God offers the hope that we might become real; that we might be defined not by the lie but by Himself; that we might live for things that are lasting and of eternal significance. God uses both pain and success to reveal the emptiness of the things of this world; that we might finally embrace things that are of true substance.

After the accident, as my worldly idols crumbled, I began to grasp some of these things for the first time. My pride and arrogance had been crushed and I began to understand and empathize with others who also suffer in this world. My pain illuminated their pain, allowing me to see beyond my selfish self. I was becoming real. In my journals I wrote:

> I fear a side effect from my fall is the ensuing pessimism which pervades my soul. It's as if God opened my eyes to the struggles which all living things endure. I now empathize with the sick, needy, dying, living in fear, and suffering... I see fate befall the huddled masses, the lonely stranger encounters its embrace. The pious kneel at their altar, while the wicked dance in their disgrace. Can you see the cries of the innocent? Can you fathom the depths of their dismay? As misfortune ensnares both the wicked and holy, and leaves us all in disarray.

As I struggled with this new paradigm, God led me to the words of Peter in the Bible:

> Therefore, since Christ suffered in his body, arm yourself also with the same attitude, because he who has suffered in his body is done with sin. As a result, he does not live the rest of his earthly life for evil human desires, but rather for the will of God. For you have spent enough time in the past doing what pagans choose to do—living in debauchery, lust, drunkenness, orgies, carousing and detestable idolatry...
> Dear friends, do not be surprised at the painful trial you are suffering, as though something strange were happening to you. But rejoice that you participate in

the sufferings of Christ, so that you may be overjoyed
when his glory is revealed.—1 Peter 4:1-6, 12-13

The Bible verse went deep to my soul and spoke directly to
me. *Rejoice that you participate in the suffering?* That was so back-
wards from what I had believed. But I had spent enough time in my
life doing what "pagans" do and I had found it void. Now I was
suffering in my body; I was suffering a painful trial and I was beginning to understand the purpose for the suffering. As such, I've come
to see the car crash as a gift, a rare window through which I was able
to experience the nature of our existence with clarity. It was a major
"wake-up call," an outside message disturbing my sleep, telling me
news of vital importance. For that I am thankful. Through the lie,
we've succumbed to spiritual ether that dulls our senses and causes us
to greatly underestimate the tactics of our foe. Only semiconscious
of the intensity and the significant ramifications of the battle, we never
fully engage. Instead we lay dormant, numb with spiritual Novocain,
vulnerable to the suggestion and insinuations of the lie that bait and
lure in the name of entertainment.

But pain and the disillusionment of worldly success break that
trance, upend our assumptions, and point us toward the edge of a new
direction for life: All we should do—all we *can* do—is seek the Lord,
that He may grant us grace in this world as we pass on to Heaven.
And if we follow His will, we shall find the rarest of all gifts... peace.
Should we find that peace, we will never want to lose it, for the only
thing eternal in life is God.

From this perspective, we can safely conclude that God cares
only about the genuine wealth of our souls and not our earthly desires
that are based on the lie. Like Moses, He has a divine plan for our
lives. What we may see as evil or empty, He is meaning for good that
we might become useful in His hands—even if it means "being beaten
into the dust" from which we came.

UNCONDITIONAL SURRENDER

At some point the dialog must cease about such things and an
honest personal assessment must begin. While the world seems to

offer so much, it's all just a fragile *personal* illusion. If *personal* peace is to be found, it certainly is not found in things such as these. This world and this life are a meaningless struggle against the inevitable. Why do you pursue the envy of others? Is not life too short to waste your time on empty pursuits?

To avoid pain is only to ignore true reality. To push on to greater and greater heights is futile. "Life" is found neither in the absence of intense pain nor in the attainment of great success. To believe so is to embrace one of the great lies of dualism, that there is some lasting value in material things alone. *Enduring peace and meaning cannot reasonably be found in things that do not last.* No one on their death bed wished they had worked more hours or acquired more things.

Soon enough, we *will* face this fact through the inevitable loss of all that the Dream Machine promotes as meaningful and valuable. We know this from the laws of physics; we know it from the ancient wisdom of those who have gone before us, and we know it in our hearts. Therefore, embracing the lie (after we recognize it for what it is) leads only to pessimism, fatalism, and even insanity as we continue to grasp at the things we can see for answers to questions that can only be found in the things that are not seen.

There comes a time, either by force or by choice, when the lie must die. The lie and its *personal* implications must be refused not just in principle, but in a *personal* volition that requires a change of course and an abandonment of specific plans and dreams in light of their futility. The only reasonable option is one of surrender, surrender to God, where we seek His ways and His face like never before, willing to accept life on His terms.

◆　◆　◆

Two months after the car accident, I was seeing little physical progress in my recovery. My soul had continued in a spiraling descent of frustration, anger, and disillusionment. It was now summer and Tiffany was planning to take the kids on her annual visit to see her family. The timing couldn't have been worse. My fears and physical pain had reached a peak and I felt I was teetering on the edge of sanity. We both knew that there was little Tiffany could do to help even if she stayed. So we agreed that she should go, leaving me alone. It was just as well. The next step in my journey was a two-person ordeal… and she wasn't one of those people.

After I dropped them off at the airport, I drove to a secluded hill overlooking the Cascade Mountains. Finding a quiet place to sit and reflect, I pulled out a personal poetry book I hadn't written in for nearly ten years. It was difficult to write—so much time had passed, so many things had changed since those years in college when everything was so clear—but as the words began to flow, my thoughts found their place.

I openly confessed to God that I was angry and frustrated. I released it all to Him, holding nothing back about what I felt and thought. It just didn't make sense to me why I had been saved in a miracle and then left to suffer. But I vowed to stop asking and accepted this as my position in life. At that moment, I chose to put my faith in God. With my head finally bowed in submission before Him, I renounced earthly pursuits and devoted my life to His Kingdom… regardless of how I felt, regardless of the circumstance, regardless of the outcome.

Exhausted by decades of self-effort, I collapsed into the arms of the One who had wounded me. I was done with the fight. With the Cascade Mountains looking on as my only witness, my heart knelt before Him and I began to embrace Him as my Lord—not joyfully, but purposefully—as one who had been conquered. I cried in surrender as all the emotions of what I had been through over the past few months were lifted from my soul. The strong-willed, stubborn child had been broken. I succumbed with whimpering and with tears—but without the energy or will to be defiant or question anymore. The white flag went up. An admission of position followed: I was weak and He was strong. He was God and I was not. My will, my preferences, and my dreams began to breathe their last. The lie had died, desire died. There was nothing left.

For the first time, I was prepared to truly seek God—not the god I had imagined or desired, but the God who truly is. Surrender has since become an ongoing process of my heart, but that day was the beginning of something new. I began to seek God not for what He could do for me, but simply because He existed and I wanted to know Him as He is.

Chapter 6

Ponder God

God is dead. God remains dead. And
we have killed him.[1]
    —Friedrich Nietzsche (1844-1900)

Nietzsche is dead. Nietzsche remains
dead.
        —God (Eternal)

A.W. Tozer once said, "What comes to our mind when we think about God is the most important thing about us."[2] That's a statement well worth consideration, for there are no thoughts greater than those we hold towards God. Our concept of God forms the pivotal reference point around which all of life revolves. God creates; God loves; God sustains; God is the source and the destination of all we seek—the peace and meaning we all desire. Our perception of God forms the mental paradigm that we use to interpret all personal experiences, giving us the context and perspective from which to live and define ourselves. The center of our worldview, the conceptual boundary of reality… our thoughts toward Him are, most certainly, "the most important thing about us."

Tozer assumes that modern humanity does, in actuality, think about God. I make no such assumption. In the constant hustle of Western life, one's mind is violently thrust about from demand to demand, the soul swept by the currents of daily obligations with little time to seek or experience peace. Moment by moment we are consumed by the world and the Machine until the days themselves slip by unnoticed. Hours upon hours pass by without pondering, without considering, without contemplating God at all.

Throughout adolescence and adult life my thoughts of God were a matter of convenience, even entertainment, as I reveled in the engrossing world of philosophy. What I did think about Him was contorted and confined; I conformed God to *my* image, rather than humbly allowing Him to conform me to His. After the accident, however—with the physical aspect of my being in such disarray and with all my idols in shambles—I had both the need and the desire to seek God anew. My universe had collapsed to the minuscule reality of an atom. All my pompous pontification and philosophical speculations had dissolved and evaporated, leaving me bare, facing the pure simplicity of a broken spirit. In my journal I wrote:

> Reality has befriended me on an island of unfulfilled dreams. I hold on to one thought, a piercing vision containing the essence of my subconscious: "We are born. We shall die. It matters not what we accomplish as long as we have found God and remain at peace with ourselves."

"As long as we have found God."—a more important search does not exist, nor could a more daunting task face mere mortals. To seek God is no arbitrary chore, but a consuming hunger that yields to no artificial fulfillment. It's a quest that requires all that we are—a passion in proportion to the desperation one derives from our intrinsic need to find Him. For in God alone shall we find the peace, meaning, and fulfillment that has eluded the mass of humanity since the earliest days of our existence.

IN THE BEGINNING

Our very existence begs the question of our origin, for everything is the result of something. (There has never been a proven exception to this basic law of physics.) Without a sense of our past we live with no reference for the present or future, aimlessly trying to seize the moment while avoiding the inevitability of death. Life and death: It's the guaranteed continuum that we see passing before us as the moments of our lives tick away. Earth, stars, trees, civilizations... all have a beginning and an end, as does all matter and energy. Intuitively we know this and instinctively we know that beyond life and death there must exist a Presence, a Passion, a Person... an original cause to all that is seen. *Who* that might be has been the innate question asked by all of humanity, the question that shouts from the core of our being.

Some seek the answer with sincerity and honesty, being true to the longings felt in their inner being. Others seek only superficially, asking the questions but dodging the Answer itself, unwilling to face the implications of finding One greater than self.

Aristotle saw the need for such a first cause.[3] Rather than embrace the possibility of God, however, he thought that the world might have emerged from energy and matter alone—though he never addressed where that energy and matter might have come from. In the thirteenth century, Thomas Aquinas developed Aristotle's ideas further, taking them to their logical conclusion. With great eloquence and a passion that emerged from his personal faith, he illuminated the physical and philosophical need for a starting point for all matter and order. By expounding on the laws of cause and effect, he logically and persuasively argued that *every* effect must have a cause. Pursuing this logic beyond the boundaries of the physical, he argued for the existence of an "uncaused cause"—a beginning to everything material caused by something immaterial. "Therefore it is necessary to admit a first effective cause," Aquinas argued, "to which everyone gives the name God."[4] For several centuries many dodged the obvious by hiding behind the limitations of the scientific method. Many claimed that the universe was eternal and in a perpetual "steady state" that had no beginning and would have no end (even though this idea is completely contrary to basic laws of thermodynamics). Early in the twentieth century technology caught up with this notion. Albert Einstein became a theist after looking through the telescope of Edwin Hubble.[5] By comparing the speeds and the distances of stars relative to each other, Hubble had traced the history of the universe back to a single point in time and space. The implications were profound: *At one point there was nothing. Then there was everything... and Something had to cause it.* It was a life-altering realization for the two men and their findings sent theological shock waves throughout the scientific community.

Profound advances in the fields of biochemistry and genetics have also shaken conventional theories of origins.[6] The sincere atheist—the one who honestly searches for truth with a mind open to the possibility of a personal creator—soon runs out of scientific reason to deny the obvious. Those who are willing to lay aside their presuppositions and allow the evidence to speak for itself often find their objections falling apart one by one—and that's when they find God.

Those who choose to deny God endure, of course, and many do so not on scientific grounds, but on moral ones. Charles Darwin hardened his heart against the Creator when his daughter died at an early age.[7] The philosopher Voltaire maintained his belief in God, but rejected organized religion due to the hypocrisy and perversion he found in the official church. Those who have experienced such pain and disillusionment know that such a reaction is more than understandable. But to conclude that God doesn't exist because "bad" things happen doesn't follow reason. One is compelled to ask them, "If God doesn't exist, why are you so angry with Him?"

At the same time, I commend the atheist for their personal honesty. Western Christianity, on the other hand, has adopted a thinly veiled atheism, living as though there were no God on a pragmatic level. For the most part, God is dead in Europe; the end of a long process of cultural diffusion, intellectual dilution, and a fading passion. Institutionalized religion squeezed God into a religious compartment until He resided only in monolithic church buildings and children's bed time stories. To a greater or lesser degree we each do the same. We have our personal thoughts about Him, but have we not compartmentalized God and contained Him in a little mental box of our own creation?

Our essential *need* for God, however, is not so easily contained. Pascal, the French physicist and philosopher said, "There is a God shaped vacuum in the heart of every man which cannot be filled by any created thing, but only by God, the Creator, made known through Jesus."[8] When pondering the yearnings of the human soul, Voltaire concluded, "If God did not exist it would be necessary to invent him."[9]

Because of our practical atheism, we are driven "to invent him" *in ourselves.* We continually seek to become that which is lacking in our perception of Him. We attempt to function as God ourselves, trying to fulfill His role in our life and in society. The consequences of these subliminal thoughts—the thoughts that drive us to act as God—pollute every aspect of our psyche. *If we don't see God for who He is, then we begin to act and think as if we are little gods; as if we are strong, as if we control our destiny.* Indeed this was the first of all temptations, the beginning of humanity's departure from the original design.[10]

As a result, we take every decision into our own hands even though we lack wisdom and insight. We carry the weight of responsibility for things we cannot control. We feel the searing burn of failure when our weaknesses are revealed. We glorify ourselves for our capabilities when we succeed.

When we compartmentalize God, we must face the "godless" places as gods ourselves. We are left alone to decide, determine, and control. By isolating ourselves from the reality of His permeating presence in all things we attempt to judge, rule, condemn, and sustain reality on our own. We might be successful to a degree, but what a terrible weight to bear—a weight with no end. We are destined to fail at such attempts. Eventually, something comes apart and the charade comes crashing down. At some point we will break, and the sooner the better. In such times we can receive the pain and suffering as a gift from God, tools in His loving hands used to shatter our false aspirations to be our own gods. Certainly suffering also comes from the natural consequences of our own waywardness, but even these seasons can be embraced as a gift of an all-loving God who beckons us back to Himself and life as He designed it.

I pity the man who "plays god" to the end, those who appear to live comfortable lives under an illusion of control. Beyond the grave, when it is too late to alter the course of their eternal journeys, they realize the error of their ways.

Prior to the accident I had been highly successful at "playing god." I now believe that is why I had to be broken down as a man. My identity had to be wiped away before I could begin to see God and seek Him for who He is. I didn't want to vary my route, but I had no choice. All my perceptions of control were ripped away. I was naked and exposed. The mirage of my strength and the façade of personal control were obliterated. In my brokenness, I came to see that safety and security are nothing but illusions. My wife, kids, job, health, sports… everything could be taken in a fleeting moment. This was a basic, but terrifying realization. I knew such things in my head, but when the truth reached my heart fear intensified beyond anything I thought possible. Everything I had thought was safe and secure under my care was now exposed, protected only by a false sense of peace that had no substance.

Through pain and suffering I fully discovered that the only way to find *true* peace on this earth is to give the control to God and trust in Him *alone*. This type of trust can be forced upon us in difficult circumstances, but it is still always a choice—a choice that can only be made from an accurate perception of who God really is. The choice is ours: will we look to our own fleeting strength and limited knowledge or will we search beyond what we can see until we find God?

KNOWING THE UNKNOWABLE

The pursuit of God eventually brings us to the edge of rational thought. Reason certainly points us in His direction but it can only take us so far. Science beckons us to search beyond the confines of the scientific method, but has limited usefulness as we seek things outside of the physical. Even the word "holy" has numerous connotations that reach far beyond the superficial, illuminating a dark chasm in under-standing. To be holy means "to be set apart," to be "unlike anything else," and to have "no comparison." God is holy in *every* sense of the word. Should we fail to understand this, we will be destined to contin-ually limit our concept of God while at the same time priding ourselves for having defined Him properly.

Human conceptual systems are built on previously developed mental constructs that allow us to make connections and comparisons with other things. If we limit ourselves to conventional thinking, we can only liken God to things we can observe by sight or touch (He is *like* a dad or *like* the air…). Or we will define God by what He is *not* (sin*less*, fault*less,* etc). But who is like Him? To what can God be compared? What reference point can be used to attempt to describe—let alone understand—this One who created all from nothing? Some understanding can be found in the very things that God has created:

> For since the creation of the world God's invisible qualities—his eternal power and divine nature—have been clearly seen, being understood through what has been made, so that they are without excuse.
> —Romans 1:20

This revelation of nature speaks loudly and clearly of the general reality of God. Though broken and distorted, nature continues to be a reflection of both His presence and His power. But beyond knowledge *about* God, where is one to go should they seek to actu-ally find such a being? A unique and special revelation of God exists in the Bible where God is revealed through the pens of the historians, poets, prophets, and apostles. Many hearts have found Him as they have contemplated the words of this book. Others have come to see Him in the very process of researching the Bible's inspiration, authen-ticity, and reliability.

Take C.S. Lewis as an example. His works of fiction have found renewed fame through the cinema portrayal of *The Lion, the Witch, and the Wardrobe* (from *The Chronicles of Narnia*—a story saturated with spiritual analogy). Lewis was not always receptive to such things. The Oxford professor became a hardened atheist by the atrocities he observed in the First World War, yet he came to a personal faith in God after carefully investigating the historical and literary credibility of the Bible. What Lewis discovered moved him beyond mere theism into a personal relationship with God through Jesus Christ. When speaking of the experience, Lewis said, "It was more like when a man, after long sleep, still lying motionless in bed, becomes aware that he is now awake."[11]

Lewis was a close friend of J. R. R. Tolkien, the creator of the *Lord of the Rings*. The two men spent countless hours together pondering God and the spiritual realities of the physical war they had endured on earth and the spiritual battles they continued to face— battles that were vividly reflected in their literary works.

Others, such as archeologist William F. Albright, came to believe in the special revelation of the Bible after verifying its historical accuracy through excavation of ancient cities and sites. In the relics and stones in the deserts of the Middle East, he found repeated confirmation of the historical accuracy of a book he had once considered fable. The book then guided him into an intimate life with God.[12]

As such, the Bible serves as a literary bridge crossing the gap between the seen and the unseen, the physical and the spiritual. In no uncertain terms, it describes the attributes of God, the One in total control of the universe. Not a molecule moves without His full awareness; not a breath is sustained without His consent. From scientific observation, Einstein concluded, "God does not play dice with the universe."[13]

To grasp the extent of God's power, one would need to grasp the full magnitude of the entire universe—both its mass and its energy. Then one would need to comprehend that after creation God had no less power at His disposal than He did before. These are the kinds of thoughts that point us toward a truer concept of God. To let the mind wander into eternity and into infinity; this is required of the one who truly wants to seek and know God. "All-powerful, all-knowing, all-present, from eternity;" these are the types of words that the Bible uses to try to describe the One who made what we see, the

One in control, the One who navigates beyond the limits of the time-space dimension.

The prophet Hosea calls us to "press on to know the Lord."[14] But who, might I ask, is equipped for such a task? With only finite, linear understanding, how could the seeker ever find Him unless He reveals Himself in tangible ways? At this point something critical separates biblical Christianity from all other expressions of faith. Other world religions seek to find God from their own understanding, defining God through their own worldview. In contrast, Christianity began when God took human form, displaying God's effort and devotion to find us. This is an infinitely distinct departure from the normal course of human religion. While humanity has sought the route that leads to God, God Himself bridged the spiritual-physical barrier by coming to earth as a man. The Christian has the audacity to claim that God stepped "over the edge" and came to earth, transcending the realm of the heavens and inhabiting the world of the material… And He did so that you might see Him, touch Him, learn from Him, and *know* Him.

Through a body of flesh and blood, He held us, comforted us, fed us, and then displayed to us the very nature of God: love. He *was* God on this earth. His movements perfectly reflected the heart of the Father, a living example and illustration of the way life was intended to be—a way completely different than that promoted by the lie—a life of service and sacrifice. Christ personified the love we all seek, *true* love that is caring, sacrificial, enduring, gracious, and great.[15]

> No one has seen God, but His only Son, who is Himself God, He has explained Him, has made Him known.
> —John 1:18 THV

Christ's ultimate display of God's love reveals no sentimental illusion. Through betrayal, beatings, and the hours that He hung bleeding in the hot sun on the cross, Jesus Christ showed us not only God, but that God is *love*. Real love. Tangible love. He displayed a love that is complete, accepting, and willing to forgive all. It's a love so unusual that the Greeks created a special word to describe it:

agape, a love given without condition or reason to those who have no claim to it. A.W. Tozer confessed his struggle to communicate the love of God with these words:

> We must try to speak of His love. All Christians have tried, but none have done it very well. I can no more do justice to that awesome and wonder-filled theme than a child can grasp a star.[16]

This kind of love can be both passionate and ferocious. When I faced the death of my desires, I had to face a love that shattered softer definitions and a God who no longer fit my conventions. His love was willing to wound me so that I might be healed. God cared enough to make me weak so that He would become strong through me. He was willing to let me see death so that I might truly live. Looking back I can see it as a profound gift, but in the moment, during the long recovery, I didn't understand. In the world we are raised and encouraged to be strong, to be independent, to control... to be like God. The accident had forced me to fully realize at least one thing: whoever I was, *I was not Him.*

PONDER GOD

"Ponder." I've said that word so many times since I was nineteen. "Philosophical," "transcendental," "metaphysical"... I once explored and stated these words with pride as if I alone understood the key to life, as if I alone knew the secret to peace and meaning. To be fair, I barely understood the meaning of them (let alone the application of them in my life). As an inquisitive youth, I understood with the utmost conjecture on how the order of things fell in my world. Dreams, illusions, mysteries... I decided what they meant and what they were. I truly felt I understood, that I had found answers through my rhetorical questioning.

But the time *must* come when philosophy gives way to reality, when all our theologizing about the nature of God gives way to speechless awe. In order to *ponder* God we must be willing to actually step over the line, discarding philosophical and intellectual pride, and placing faith in the one true God alone for enlightenment. In the secret quiet places of the heart; that's where we transcend physical limitations. When we are in the quiet place, silent and still, that's when fear and stress are shed like an unwanted coat in the spring, when we can rest in the warm rays of the sun after a long winter.

To this end, the one with an over abundance of information is at a disadvantage when compared to the one who simply searches with his soul. Saturated with knowledge and the words of others, the theologian wrestles with the most important ideas in the universe. Conversely, the shepherd gazes into the universe through the stars at night and contemplates the growth of the grasses by day. In the silence he feels the reality of God resonating in his senses, true intimacy with the Creator is ignited—an awareness more tangible than anything that can be touched or tasted… and in those moments, the simple man finds rest and peace for his soul.

So sacred is this relational union with God that Satan devises strategies to divert it. While some see spiritual distraction as a side effect of worldly pursuits, I see it as an integral part of Satan's intent. Packed schedules and unending demands are the hallmark struggles of the masses in the modern age, leaving no natural time or energy to truly ponder God. Words penned prior to my accident reveal my struggles in this area:

> Where has the time gone? How shall I be rewarded? Time has passed and here I lie, pondering my past and looking into the future. Have I lost the soul searching of my youth? To a lesser extent the answer is "yes." The question then is *why* was it lost? The answer is that I no longer have the time to gaze and think of nothing. At all times it is family, work, or working out. Even at night I think about the things I must do. I read business articles instead of philosophy. I study stock quotes and calculate my net worth instead of asking the simple questions. I am happy and content with my life, for I have been truly blessed. But there are times—like now—when I realize I've lost a small part of me along the way. At some point I need to walk

away from this charade and regain my quest to see God's face on this earth. To ponder God is to ponder the essence of our being; to see into the light, the breath that saves us all.

Can I suggest that the key to truly finding God may lie in doing *less* rather than *more*? The lie and the constant drone of the Dream Machine are constantly pushing us to do more, to get more, to be more—but what a farce that is. In the simplicity of unencumbered thought the mind can see more clearly, the soul can contemplate more honestly, and the brain can process sensory input more accurately. To ponder we must find a place and a space and a time to stop, think, and consider life. To ponder God we must remove ourselves from the things that Satan uses to distract us from Him, things like the TV, radio, phone, the voices of others, and the physical needs that devour our attention. Even books, meetings, and music *about* God can feed us excessively and distract us *from* God. In most cases we need contemplation far more than we need more information.

We have been chasing fulfillment in the wrong places, searching for peace and meaning at a pace that nears insanity. Humanity has constructed its own reality and we must in some measure remove ourselves from it if we are to have focused thought about God and uninterrupted communion with Him. It's finally time to recognize the pathetic nature of our accomplishments and efforts and how infinitesimally insignificant they are in comparison to all He is. In the relative newness of the industrial and technical age, we move in urban landscapes constructed in right angles, confined in boxes made by human hands, and the unrelenting schedule of society. God is not reflected in such artificial spaces. He is so much better contemplated in wild, wide-open places where the winds blow freely without boundaries, where time stands still long enough for us to breathe and rest and think. The still voice of God is so much more easily discerned in the quiet—be it in the trees of a forest or in a dim room with eyes closed and prayers opened up, the soul able to listen and receive, meditating on Truth. Certainly, all we seek must eventually permeate our lives through the heart—not just through the brain, saturated as it is with so many other concerns. Could it be that God is quietly and patiently seducing *you* to just simply, stop, rest, and just *be* with Him?

"Be still and know that I am God,"[17] the Almighty commands. It's time to rest, to think, to breathe. The time has come to cease striving and stop long enough to ponder God. Nothing could be more important.

To ponder God, in truthful meditation… that's when you become one—not with yourself, but with Him, bringing a taste of the spiritual realm into the physical world. Silence, prayer, the resonating truths of the Bible, meditation, walks that take us away from the convoluted norms of the world and the Machine… each has the potential to reach across the artificial boundaries of dualism, bringing self and God together in the present. It's a bridge to be crossed not by drugs, not by fame, nor possessions, but by a gift of God—the gift of Himself through His Son.

God is. He has reached across to you. He is reaching out now. It's your move; should the step be taken in His direction, God will respond as promised, again stepping over the edge and revealing the things of eternity to your thirsty soul in the midst of your desert.

Know God in the most provocative sense of the word.

Embrace spiritual realities in this unreal world.

From the depth of your soul, *ponder* God.

Chapter 7

Perception of Self

> What one human being can be to
> another is not a very great deal; in the
> end everyone stands alone; and the
> important thing is, who it is that stands
> alone.[1]
>
> –Arthur Schopenhauer

Pondering the God and Creator of the universe is absolutely essential if we are to discover the essence of life. Beyond this, if we desire to find our specific place in that life, then it becomes imperative that we try to define and capture who *we* are even as we ponder who He is. From our perceptions of God every other experience is interpreted. He is the eternal centrality of life, the beginning and the end of all, *including us*. Only in proper relation to Him can we discover a proper concept of "self." This discovery must be made in extreme humility, recognizing the limitations of our understanding of God, for our understanding is infinitesimally small compared to who He is. But seek ourselves we must. There is no other way to progress in the journey. Using God as a reflection point, we must turn the mirror upon ourselves and contemplate who it is that is looking back.

The quest to find self has a grand history. Those with the means and the time to wander the world continue to search for who they might be, hoping to "find themselves" somewhere where they currently are not. Others seek the wisdom of the sage; some consult the New Age channeler looking for clues from the past to help them make sense of who they are in the present and where they might find their place in the future.

Who are you? Does anyone seek self-definition anymore? The days slip by in the current of modern culture with only sporadic opportunities for self-reflection. Now and then we seem to find a temporary window, a momentary view of existence behind the veil of the material where we catch a glimmer of who we might actually be: images that stun us with simplicity, vibrant epiphanies where the real becomes momentarily "super-real," rare moments that ignite the conscience. The moment is often extinguished as fast as it came and I fear those moments themselves are few, far between, and fleeting. I've come to savor these moments in my own life. I see them from time to time in society when the masses themselves are silenced in the shadow of greater realities: 9/11, the death of a loved one, the color of the sky reflected in the waters of a deep lake… One night I saw it in a group of people assembled on a bridge, watching an explosion of fireworks in the night sky:

> For a moment,
> Just a single moment, the masses became aware of their existence.
> They caught a glimpse of the ethereal plain and understood the oneness of life.
> As the masses drifted away, I realized the consciousness they had attained was as fleeting as their knowledge of life.
> For life's perception was once again isolated to that of singularity.
> But for a sheer moment, a metaphysical instant,
> They saw what life was… and forgot.

The mental and emotional demands and the time constraints of modern life may indeed be part of the grand conspiracy, a strategy of Satan's design that distracts us to no end. Our society makes it nearly impossible to be contemplative. The media barrage continually turns our head away from more important things. It numbs us by its constant din until we are deaf to quieter, more subtle influences softly beckoning us to stop and ponder things of deep and eternal significance. Are our schedules a byproduct of contemporary life or a strategic extension of evil? God Himself only knows. But who has even five minutes a day to look in the mirror and ask, "Who am I, really?"

Instead, we are immersed, saturated, and bombarded with message after message telling us that we must become something else in order to become something of value. The Western mirror of self-definition has been severely contorted by the lie. Defined by what we have, what we do, and how we look, the image of self that is projected back by the world leaves us feeling inadequate and incomplete. By default we accept this image and measure ourselves in contrast to the standards of the media elite. A few will instinctively rebel against this status quo by going "alternative." But even these will find themselves defined by the very alternatives they attempted to embrace to show their uniqueness.

In either case the question of "self" is relegated to the arbitrary and whimsical notions of humanity—people trying to define people, trying to create their own identity, defining themselves by external aspects (race, nationality, neighborhood, car they drive), community affiliations (college, sports, clubs, group memberships), and political interests instead of who they really are if those things were stripped away. With no hope of answers that satisfy, and with the numbing effects of the lie, man retreats into resolve—what Henry David Thoreau called "lives of quiet desperation."[2] Panic, anxiety, depression, disillusionment… these are just a few of the symptoms of our silent desperation.

To find a way out, some make a calculated departure from the norm, looking for a circumstantial change that will bring a sense of direction and purpose. The man in mid-life crisis, searching for self in the arms of a younger woman; the mother, clinging to the control of her children as they slip away into adulthood; the teen, shopping through an unending sea of musical options, trying to find something that will both set them apart and simultaneously identify themselves with others. In such seasons of "quiet desperation" I often turned to my journal, finding a place where my thoughts and feelings could make sense of themselves:

> Where has the poetry gone? How has my life changed? The years of striving under all of which we measure success has taken its toll on my creative soul. It is true what Solomon said, "Meaningless, Meaningless, everything is meaningless." So how may I regain my inquisitive soul? Or has my soul been lost among the advanced degrees and the responsibility of fatherhood? It is the way of the world. Yes, I have succumbed to the suburban dream and lost my own. I know now my dream was a distorted view of reality, but through that distortion I viewed life with awe and clarity.

> As a man I have put away childish things, and in the process lost my innocence—an innocence I cannot even vaguely remember. To play with my children, Jake and Audrey, brings back my inner self; it fills my soul and reminds me of what I have lost. I feel I have sacrificed my inner "inquisitive youth" to gain this outward life…

IDENTITY LOST AND FOUND

To truly find our place in life, our concept of self must be consistent with truth. The more our perception of self aligns with *actual* reality, the clearer our vision becomes and the more wisdom enters into our thinking and decisions. At the very dawn of humanity, man and woman existed in perfect harmony with God. These essential ingredients of life were found in the purity of original creation in a moment by moment walk with the Creator. Naked and without shame the man and the woman walked in unity with God. It was not to last. Just as he does today, Satan tempted Adam and Eve with the physical. He offered them an apple along with the promise that if they should eat it, they could "become as God."[4] Adam and Eve took the bait, the first of all humans to make the mistake. This most basic of temptations has been our continual downfall ever since. It's even the temptation that Satan and many of his fellow angels embraced when they rebelled against God and tried to take God's place of glory. The rebellion failed and Satan and the other fallen angels (demons, as we know them today) were banned from heaven. Today they roam the earth seeking still to rob God of your soul and to destroy those who believe in Him.[5]

Moment by moment the battle rages—Satan's lies versus God's truth—and in the balance hangs our perception of our very identity, our perception of self.

SOMEONE, BUT IN WHOSE EYES?

As in the quest to find God, the quest to find self demands thought, thought on a different level. We must be introspective, attempting to see ourselves as God Himself sees us. We must see things as they *are*, before determining *what might be.*

Consider this: *humanity, by default, defines itself not in relation to God, but in relation to others.* We attempt to find our place, our roles, and our purposes by comparing and contrasting our lives with those around us. But to find life's worth in others is a departure from God. The emptiness is self-evident; the justification for such comparisons arbitrary and unstable. So why do we hold our souls up to the scrutiny of others? Do we really want to hear what others have to say? Why should we care about their arbitrary opinions? Life is too short and the gift is too beautiful to waste it worrying about the judgment of others. Yet without a conscious option for determining who we really are, our perceptions of how others perceive us drive us and consume us moment by moment, day by day until a lifetime is consumed by the expectations of others.

If we are to find ourselves in the minds of others (our image versus our true character), we allow them to control our inner identities—a dangerous and precarious place to put our soul. Yet this is the primary "default setting," the automatic point of reference we use to try to determine who we are and what our value might be. The implications of this reverberate continually as we appeal to the affections of these surrogate gods.

If we are to find our identity in others we must question the totality of the human race—a formidable task that must take into account each individuals standards and expectations. We become the actors, the whole world our audience, with the whims and desires of the many becoming isolated on our shoulders. The burden is insanely heavy and the script becomes phenomenally complicated. And when the final curtain is drawn shut, we will find that the audience cared for nothing but their own temporary satisfaction at our expense.

The lie must be rejected. Truth must be sought. We must ponder God and find our identity and place in His eternal order. Only there may we find peace.

THE ONLY ONE WHO MATTERS

In the search for self, it matters not who we are in the eyes of other humans—the masses who wander as we do, trying to find their place. The things they pursue, the worldly lies that permeate their pursuit of the material… these things have no ability to transcend into the spiritual and tell us who we are. But to be rightly related to God, to understand our identity in the One central to *all* reality—would not His perspective affect the *whole* of our self-concept, and should not His definition of us be the standard by which we define ourselves?

> You must look beyond what we know or feel outwardly.
> There-in doth soul's touch, free to play in light of such.
> Perceptions attained on a different plain,
> Life and understanding—only known to God.

God's movements toward us began in His thoughts during eternity past. His intentions became clear through the creation of the time-space dimension upon which He set the stage for everything to follow. For thousands of years humanity navigated throughout history with the sporadic inspiration of God's prophets and the written accounts of His actions. For generations the prophecies held out hope for a coming salvation, an intervention into human history like no other. Jesus Christ was that intervention. When God stepped across the perceived spiritual/physical barrier, He "became flesh and lived among us."[6] With His very being, Christ crossed the boundaries of the heavens and took His place among humanity, making His grand entrance as a vulnerable newborn. The possibility of such a move by deity was rejected by the religious elite of Israel, but the simple masses embraced it *and they found themselves in it.*

History from this point on held remarkable possibilities that forever changed the way that humanity might experience God and experience themselves in Him. The life of Christ marked a fundamental shift in the nature of the quest for life and meaning. Religious efforts have forever emphasized what we must do to embrace spiritual realities. But now God had entered our reality in graphic defiance of the imagined barrier between the physical and the spiritual. "For the Law was given through Moses, but God's unfailing love and faithfulness came through Jesus Christ," wrote John. "No one has ever seen God. But His only Son, who is Himself God, inseparable from the Father, He has shown God to us."[7]

The audacity of such a claim has divided humanity into two camps ever since: those who believe and those who do not. Christ Himself spoke of it in no uncertain terms. He claimed to *embody* that which others only spoke about, claiming not that He *knew* the way out of the desert, but that He *was* the way out of the desert: "I am the way and the truth and the Life. No one comes to the Father but through Me,"[8] He said.

The implications of such claims astounded some and appalled others. *Ultimate Truth was not a concept, but a Person. To find Truth (and therefore to find self) one must find Him or forever wander fatherless in the dry sands.* To claim to be the way, the Truth, and the life is one thing… to actually be so is quite another. Christ did so, but not as some sort of example or to prove something to someone. His life was a pure and natural extension of who He knew Himself to be—no pretense, no looking over His shoulder to see who was watching. His identity was intact, as was the purpose to which He had been called. He had come—He *has* come—to find the souls who recognize their "lostness" and are willing to be led out of the desert into a transformed life.

His purpose was not without price; it required the ultimate sacrifice of His life. At this point the Westerner often stumbles, since the concept of sacrifice is largely foreign to cultures that were once built on Christian realities but have since lost this foundation. Most Westerners neither understand the need nor the means of reconciliation with God. These things are still intuitively understood by the Hindu and the Muslim who recognize the sinful separation between a holy God and the prideful independence of humanity. Their religions—their attempts to appease God—are laced with continual sacrifice as they try to reconcile themselves to God in light of the pending punishment for our insurrection and our attempts to become like God ourselves.

Christ's sacrifice marked the end of such attempts. He revealed the lie, broke the cycle, and looked into the eyes of those yearning for peace and love and said, "It is finished. Forgiveness is at hand. It can be well with your soul again."[9] Because of what He did, we can stop doing. We can come to Him and just be with Him again, embracing the forgiveness that cost Him everything yet is given to us freely and without condition.

I had read about God's forgiveness as a child and understood it only as a child with a pure heart can. Only after leaving my Christian faith in pursuit of the world did I begin to understand the *need* for forgiveness. After more than a decade of partying and searching for peace and meaning in a world without God, I fully felt the emotions of guilt and shame—emotions from past actions that can consume someone's lost soul. Over the years I continually asked for forgiveness, but I did so still clinging to the guilt of the sin I had committed.

The feelings followed me every day until the accident and miracle at Joshua Tree. After being discharged from the hospital that night we returned to the vacation house we were renting in Palm Springs. I had a very difficult sleep, my body trying to fend off the shock and trauma of the day's events. When I woke the next morning, the first thing I wanted to do was see my face and my body. I hobbled slowly to a full-length mirror in the hallway; reflected back was a bruised and mangled face. It should have been a shocking and repulsive sight, but an entirely different emotion flooded over me: All I felt was complete and absolute forgiveness of every sin I had committed in my life. I felt 100 percent in my soul that I had died at Joshua Tree the day before, that God saved me from death, and that all the sins of my past were forgiven. Imagine, a lifetime of sin wiped away, the chalkboard of the soul absolutely clean, the freedom to start a new life, seeing the world as an adult, but with the cleansed soul of a child.

I knew this emotion was a gift from God. How else could I have looked at my mangled face and felt absolute peace and forgiveness? I didn't ask to feel that way; I didn't know I could feel this way, but I believe this is God's intention for all of us—a complete confirmation of His forgiveness of our sins. Those who have allowed Christ into their lives are now identified with Him. The Bible tells us that if you believe in Christ you have *died*. You have been *killed* in the flesh. By God's grace you have been *raised* from death. By His blood you have been *cleansed* and *forgiven*. By His grace and by His Spirit you have been given *new life.*[10] This is the grand reality for all who have placed their souls in His care. The man in my mirror was a graphic reflection of who we all are, whether we feel like it or not. For some reason, He allowed me to feel it at that moment.

Prior to Joshua Tree and the car accident, my identity had been based on the lie… and the lie had imprisoned me and would have killed me one way or the other. Who I had perceived myself to be was a complete departure from who God had *already* made me to be. I had been trying to be something I was not, living contrary to the reality of Christ in me. The wave of truth that washed over me as I looked in the mirror was clear and full of emotion, similar to the experience that some have when they renounce the lie and bend their knees before God for the first time. I felt it, but then I went on with life as I had known it, as if I could still be the same even though I was different.

It took the force of the car crash five weeks later to begin the stripping process, the brutal tearing away of the false sense of self that was so imbedded in my identity. My idols of power, control, appearances, acceptance of others… it all had to die. No longer would God allow me to define myself by other human beings. It was all to be about Him.

I believe this to be a critical crossroad in the journey from the desert. Everyone, it seems, must come to this place, though each arrive there differently. The lies that have distorted your perception of self are different from mine. The experiences that have contorted your psyche have formed idols of a different shape in your soul. All must be broken. Desire must die. Religion must die. The importance of others' perceptions of us must die… *self must die.* Only in this continual experience of stripping of lies can self be found, for only in the truth of Him can we discover who we really are.

EMBRACING SPIRITUAL REALITY IN AN UNREAL WORLD

Nine months after the accident, I went on a business trip to Southern California. It was my first major business trip since my life had been so seriously shaken. In all honesty, I really didn't want to be there. I was doing my best to fight off a barrage of fears. I was still very fragile, both inside and out. I had succumbed to a second respiratory illness and I still had head issues. From my hotel in Santa Monica, I decided to go walk on the beach, seeking solitude from my fears. With each step, however, my equilibrium was thrown off as I felt the shifting of the sand beneath my feet. I was again reminded of how vulnerable and weak I was, for even simple movement like walking on the sand was very difficult. I pressed on. It was the end of the day and the sun was beginning to set over the ocean. To the rhythm of the pounding waves and with each footstep I contemplated God, self, and all that had taken place between us. I had put aside the "why" question months before on the hillside overlooking the Cascades, but the question surfaced again as I walked slowly in the sands. "Why had all this happened? Why do I still suffer? What meaning could it possibly have?"

I found a high spot on the sand close to the waves and sat down. For months I had been praying and asking, seeking insight into what I was going through. There just had to be a purpose behind what had happened. God had clearly intervened in Joshua Tree. For some reason He had altered natural law milliseconds before I hit the rocks, saving my life. But then, only weeks later, I had my life shattered in a minor car accident? It just didn't make sense. So I asked "why?" again, but this time almost rhetorically, not expecting an answer, not expecting that there *was* an answer. But unlike before, when the question was answered with silence, this time it all came together. All the pieces of the past and the present merged in to a single picture and I could at last see why.

I had once walked in innocent Truth as a child. Through ignorance and choice, I had abandoned Truth at age sixteen and exchanged it for the lie. The lie had deeply entwined itself in my heart. On the rocks of Joshua Tree and through the car accident, I had been both killed and given new life. Satan had tried to destroy, but God was using it for good, forcing me to see who He had made me to be, giving me the opportunity to discover who I truly was beyond the physical lies I had embraced. He destroyed my ability to do the worldly things I once placed so much value in. He broke me of my past, freed me of the earthly chains that I once clung to. He had tested my faith in order to make me strong—not strong in myself, but strong in Him. Everything I went through was to destroy what I had become and let me see the world as I once did. And it all occurred to bring me back to my childhood innocence of God.

Words that I had written in my journal nearly a decade before had become realized:

> Feel the freedom of a cleansed soul. And see life as a child, devoid of its toilsome toll.

I had to die to self before I could find myself in Him. It had to happen this way; I know it had to happen this way. There *is* no other way. I was so stubborn I had to be broken before I could realize who I was. God had to shatter who I believed myself to be before I saw the need to shed the lies. He had to break my will before I would be willing to begin to embrace who He had made me to be. I had been reduced to a child, because at the core of my essence I *am* a child; a child of the living and personal God.

As the sun was setting on the ocean, I became aware of a stirring from deep inside my spirit—the Holy Spirit—a feeling I had not felt in eighteen years. The feeling pulled me back in time nearly two decades, back to the days when I walked this same shore as a child. I had grown up near Laguna Beach, just south of where I now sat. Back then, I would walk on the beach in youthful wonder, pondering God and feeling His presence. Over the years, and engrossed in the world, I had forgotten this feeling. So many decisions, so much time had passed, but God had brought me back. He had brought me back to this beach to give me back the childlike spiritual awareness I once had.

All had transpired to show me who I was. He had brought me full circle—wiser and more humble than before—back to the place where I once knew who I was. He was my Father. I was His child. In relation to Him I saw myself for who I was again. And as an extension of that identity, I knew what I was to do: I was to rest in His arms, listen to His voice, and allow Him to be the very breath of all I am.

I sat quietly on the beach letting Truth soak back into my soul. I had picked up several shells and had been shifting them back and forth in my hand. God led me to take the shells and make a cross out of them; one by one I pressed them into the sand. It was a symbol, just as the cross has been for centuries—a symbol of death and new life, a symbol of purpose and direction. But between God and I that evening, it was even more than that; it was a sign. The shells were to me as Noah's rainbow was to him: a sign of God's promise. I had traveled a long way with still a long way to go; He was healing me and transforming me, shaping me into the image of His Son, but He made it clear to me that evening that He would not put me through this type of trauma again.

There were, however, mountains yet to climb—one big mountain in particular.

Chapter 8

Overcome Fear

God is the God of Truth. He is in reality. He is in the now; but in the domain of fear the mind is projected into the future. In the future the mind is alone and isolated from the ever-present God of the here and now.

—Malcolm Smith

There is no fear in love, but perfect love casts out fear.[1]

—The Apostle John

It is never fun to realize that you're not God... not at first, at least. When the veil is lifted on our identity, revealing that we are but children in an angry world, the entire paradigm of life must be restructured. As perceptions adjust to reality, the soul can be thrown into confusion, uncertainty, concern... into fear. I know. I've been there. I still go there. After the car accident, fear had become all too real, all too powerful, all too present in the inner confines of my heart. Subconsciously I had believed that I was a little god, in control of my destiny. As circumstances crumbled, the things I had unknowingly trusted for security and purpose were blowing in the dust. As I wrestled with the loss of who I was, fear tormented me daily.

Part of the struggle was physical. My brain had been shaken seriously. It seemed like my brain now floated freely in a pressurized water balloon within my skull. I felt that it could all explode without warning. I couldn't look up at all. Any lateral twisting of my neck sent everything spinning, as did bending over and the slightest bit of vertical movement. All I could do was walk, and even that I could not do very well. The physique I had worked so hard to develop rapidly atrophied through inactivity. As my body image deteriorated, so did my self-image. I felt weak, so very weak in body, mind, and spirit.

Much of the fight was mental as I came to grips with the true limitations of my fragile mortality. The smallest of deviations in my routine sent me tumbling into anxiety. All I could do was drive directly to work and back; any slight detour from my established commute made my heart beat harder, my breath hard to catch. The humility was stunning. I was no longer the tough guy; I was terrified by the smallest of challenges. I had always considered fearful individuals as pathetic, undisciplined, and frail. Now I was one of them and I judged myself just as I had judged them. It was all gone; in every way I was little more than a tattered shell of my former self-perception. I was being incarcerated by fear. But somewhere deep inside the instinct to live still burned; the desire to be free flickered like a candle in the breezes of circumstance. To stay in such a fearful place would be my eventual death, and so I purposed to push through and rid myself of the prison. I had to face the fear.

At first it took all of my energy just to leave the house. Each step away from the door required an intense mental process. Slowly I ventured onto the sidewalks of my neighborhood, step by step, carefully avoiding the cracks. I ventured out alone, not wanting to trust on anyone but God. It was my own personal desert and I needed to learn to stand alone again. Everything had to be relearned: physically, mentally, emotionally. I was learning to walk again; every step and stumble accompanied by vivid fears of the known, fears of the unknown, and fears of vulnerability to unseen foes... the same foes who had their way with me in Joshua Tree.

Placing one foot in front of the other, left foot, right foot, then left again… every step was deliberate, every step had to be based on trust and humility—things I never had to depend upon before. Progress was measured in minutes and inches. As I walked in the neighborhood, I daily pushed a little longer, a little farther through the fear.

During this season, my wife had ordered a set of tapes from a British Christian speaker named Malcolm Smith. One of the tapes was on fear and its message illuminated my plight like the vibrant blast of a warship's searchlight. I thought I was alone, but this man understood me. He knew what I was facing. He felt it and identified with it, yet he showed no sympathy or condolence. Anointed and eloquent, his words resonated with Truth through his thick English accent. For months his exposition of simple biblical principles became my daily briefing, a continual verbal infusion of Truth that began to replace the years of lies. I listened to the tape every day when I drove to and from work, a commute that lasted 35-40 minutes each way. While listening to the tape, I pondered God and self. The principles slowly established a new cadence for the new life ahead. It was nothing less than a reprogramming of my mind. Fear had imprisoned my thoughts, and I knew that I must voluntary and intentionally adjust my thinking to let go of the fear—or go insane. I listened to the tape so much that I memorized every word, even mimicking his English accent. There were two Bible verses that Malcolm Smith referenced in the tape that particularly resonated in my soul, retraining my mind and my body to this new rhythm of life:

Be anxious for nothing, but in everything, through prayer and supplication with thanksgiving, let your request be made known to God. And the peace of God, which surpasses all comprehension, shall guard your hearts and your minds in Christ Jesus.
—Philippians 4:4

Even though I walk through the valley of the shadow
of death, I will fear no evil, for You are with me.
—Psalm 23:4

I was rediscovering life as a child, doing it all for the first time
again—senses fully alive, taking nothing for granted. I was bridled by
the immediate demands of the next step, never focusing beyond where
I was. And most of all, I was learning to give the control of my life
into God's hands. I was learning to trust Him instead of relying on
my feeble strength.

One day as I walked cautiously around my neighborhood, I
looked off in the distance, resting my eyes on Mt. Si, the dominant
peak in the distance, one that I had ascended before my accident. I
remember thinking that I may never climb that mountain or any other
mountain again. But then a sentence popped in my head—an
implanted thought, as if I were reading invisible words before my
eyes: *you will climb Mt Si.* The thought shocked me. Mt. Si domi-
nated the horizon above my neighborhood, located miles to the east
of Seattle near the Cascade Mountain foothills. It stands as an
imposing monolith, rising 4,000 vertical feet from its base. The
roundtrip hike is eight miles, steep, and full of switchbacks. I had
climbed it once before the accident, when I was in great shape, and it
exhausted me then. Your legs burn on the way up and feel like rubber
on the way down. To think I could climb it after my accident, with my
physical limitations and fears, was a preposterous thought. At the time
I was doing my best to walk thirty minutes on flat sidewalks without
losing my balance or my mind. It seemed impossible, but the call was
clear. God had raised the bar; my physical recovery was now being
paralleled by a formidable inner challenge that surpassed the heights
of Mt. Si. The biggest mountain yet to climb was in my soul; the
mountain of fear. I accepted the challenge and set my sights on both
mountains.

One day months later I took my son with me on my walk
through the neighborhood. At one point, I saw a trail in the woods. I
knew this was the nature trail surrounding our master-planned
community, but did not know how long it was or where it got out. We

lived in Snoqualmie, a small city just east of downtown Seattle and very close to the Cascade Mountains. It was more country than city, with huge areas of northwest wilderness right out our back door. In our neighborhood, we had mountain lion and black bear sightings, and a wild elk herd would often visit our valley. Therefore, to go off and explore the nature trail was to go off and enter the deep woods of the Northwest. We decided to explore it. I didn't think it could be too long or too difficult, but I was wrong.

We followed the trail down steep switchbacks into the beautiful forest. Ancient trees towered above us; ferns covered the forest floor. As we reached the bottom of the half mile descent, I realized that my head couldn't take the strenuous climb back up the switchbacks. The head pressure would've been too much for me. I decided to continue on the path, thinking that it would eventually come out somewhere else in the neighborhood. The further we went, however, the more uncertain I became. Panic started to set in. I didn't know what to do. I couldn't go back, but I didn't know where the trail was going either. I was lost! Adrenaline surged into my veins. Anxiety spiraled out of control. I had to sit down in the middle of the trail, sweat beading down my clammy face.

"Are you okay, Daddy? Are you okay?" Jake asked cautiously, not sure he wanted to know the answer. The fear now took on an accusing tone. *It's not just you out here. You've led your son into your nightmare. Nice work. What were you thinking?!* I took a few controlled breaths and tried to focus. *Even though I walk through the valley of the shadow of death, You are with me. Even though I walk through the valley of the shadow of death, You are with me. Even though…*

"Yea, I'm okay Jake. Just resting a bit," I said as my thoughts reassembled themselves in light of God's presence. *Narrow the options down to one. Press on or go back?* Too embarrassed to call for help on my cell phone (admitting that I had again led my son into danger) and without the strength to climb back out the steep path, I decided to press on. Within a mile we started to get our bearings and eventually we exited the forest on the far side of the neighborhood. I was shocked how far we had walked. Exhausted physically and mentally, I pushed my pride aside and called Tiffany to pick us up and bring us home. Not until much later did I share with her the battle that had taken place in my mind.

After the hike that day, I decided I needed to face my fears, and to face them alone in the woods. The root of my fears was very clear: I had lived under the illusion of control for almost twenty years, automatically taking charge of my circumstances and destiny in every situation rather than trusting God. After my accident, I realized that in one instantaneous second anything can be ripped away from us. *Control was an illusion* and when I realized this, it devastated my entire worldview. But I knew I had to face it. I decided to intentionally place myself into situations that scared me mentally and challenged me physically in order to cleanse my body and soul of the fear.

The Northwest woods are incredibly beautiful. Ancient and dark, the temperate rainforest is a sight all of us should see once in a lifetime. It's also an intimidating world if you are alone. Because of the bears and mountain lions authorities never recommended hiking alone. Given my current mental state and physical limitations it wasn't the safest choice, but it was the one thing that would absolutely force me to trust in God.

The hikes became the building blocks of a new life; life beyond the lie of self-sufficiency and personal control. Symbolically and actually, they were journeys into a more dependent, more integrated experience with God. Through the shadows of the ferns and giant trees, I walked alone with Him. During the first few weeks I was so afraid that I would continually recite the two Bible verses from the Malcolm Smith tape. I was fragile, I was fearful, and I lacked trust in God. The first walks were limited to twenty minutes roundtrip. As my strength increased so did the duration of the hikes. Removed from any semblance of the manmade world, I could ponder God and the beauty of His creation, and I began to selfishly relish this time alone with Him. The forest was my crucible, burning away my control issues and allowing me to understand what it means to trust in God. I had been led to the wilderness to escape my desert.

THE VALLEY DEFINED

Like the talons of an unseen raven, fear descends upon the soul as a shadow. Chronic worry incapacitates and paralyzes in its attack, devouring any semblance of creative, energetic living. It robs us of vision and peace, sucking life from both the body and the soul, choking out any sense of intimacy with the Father. Sometimes building upon itself in rapid succession, unchecked fear can escalate into panic and attacks of anxiety that engulf the mind in a swirling tornado of disconnected, unreal thoughts. Like the colors of a demented rainbow, fear manifests itself in many hues, emanating from a myriad of possible stimuli. Finances, illness, human rejection, loss of loved ones; the catalysts for anxiety know no limits.

Fear never travels alone. With fear come other companions from the darkness—associates that cause widespread chaos and disarray. Anger, frustration, and manipulation emanate from fearful hearts; self-pity and a victim mentality incapacitate the will. Envy, gossip, and self-

> Only those who risk going too far can possibly find out how far one can go.
> —T.S. Eliot

ishness infest relationships. Isolated in the valleys of fear, the strength of the soul is neutralized as the shadows of mountains cast long fingers of darkness through the heart.

The journey from the desert, by its very nature, leads us through such valleys, places where our fears must be exposed in their raw nakedness and faced with faith and trust. Mountains like Si stand immovable in the path of every human, intimidating, daunting, and taunting—demanding decision from each of us. Does one move beyond the worry and push through fear? Or does one resign them self to the confines of the prison?

THE ROOTS OF FEAR

Fear is a hideous extension of the dualistic worldview. What we fear is the loss of the things Satan promises through the world. Finances, relationships, position, power, recognition, health, comfort, control, adventure… these things were never created to take the place of God in the human psyche; yet these are the things to which we cling to in fleeting desperation.

As such, worry can be a valuable messenger, telling us when and where we still embrace the materialistic lie; the lie that says one's essence, value, and security come from what one has, what one does, and what one looks like. Difficult circumstance or the mirage of success, however, cast light into the shadows of the lie, revealing the things we are trusting in as fragile illusions. Such revelations ignite our fears, fears in proportion to our dependence upon these false gods.

In expectant hope of holding on to such things, many are drawn into a twisted faith, searching for the religious formula that will persuade God to protect and preserve the objects of the lie. We pray, we plead, we obey, and we serve; offering up sacrifices of our own making to God, hoping that if we do *our* part, He will be appeased and give us the very things that Satan uses to lure us away from intimacy and dependence upon Him (something to think about!). When we place our faith in the material, we fear—quite correctly—that He has little respect for the most precious of worldly things and that He will eventually strip them from the clutches of our hands. Sooner or later, be it now or at the moment of death, He will ensure that the objects of our desire will be destroyed until we seek nothing but Him.

IN PERSPECTIVE

Fear can only be fully understood when it is seen in relation to God. As the centrality of all things true and real, God graphically reveals fear for what it is. The one who desires to understand fear must again ponder God.

Contemplate this carefully: God is. He is all-knowing, powerful, and good. He is ever present, there is nowhere in reality that you can go where He is not. Furthermore, His attributes are entirely inconsistent with fear. If He is indeed all-knowing, all-powerful, loving, and good, then one *never* needs to fear that circumstances are out of His merciful control.

So in order for the mind to enter into the domain of fear, it must imagine a place where God does not exist... and such a place does not exist in the here and now. As the mind enters the domain of fear, it enters into an *imaginary* world, a world where His goodness, His strength, and His sovereignty do not exist. This is one of the most sinister aspects of the lie of dualism, drawing us into a terrifying godless illusion. Consider these words of Malcolm Smith:

> Fear indicates that by the imagination we have entered into a non-existent world. No angel is there and God Himself cannot be there because He only exists in reality. When I fear, I imagine I'm going into a land that does not exist, it is the real "Never Never Land." It doesn't exist… It's all fantasy, a lie.
>
> The magic password into this unreality are the words, "What if…?" *What if, What if?* Turn the key and you enter a Disneyland of Apocalypse Now. It's always a nightmare world. We never think the nice things. It's only a nightmare where there is no God and no angels.

In this domain of fear we use our God-given imagination, but it leads to distorted evil conclusions. Rarely do things materialize as we imagine them. In the realm of fear God is somewhere else, confined in a compartment of dualism that we have concocted in our own minds. We forget that God is in control of our lives. We believe that we are alone and we need to work out our own plan to preserve the things we feel are essential to our existence, the things of the lie.

Fear is a denial of the reality of God in the here and now. Fear is a rejection of who we are in God. This is no small matter; this is adherence to the lie and surrender to all that Satan desires to accomplish. To embrace fear is to embrace the imaginary as reality. As Smith says, "When we find these hurts and grief that usually belong to the world, if I find them in my life, it's because momentarily at least, I have forgotten that God loves me the way He does."

THE HIKE OUT

Breaking out of fear requires a rebellion of the first order. We must attack the lies with Truth, reclaiming the reality of God in the mind:

> Do not fear, *for I am with you*; do not anxiously look
> around, for I am your God and I will strengthen you.
> —Isaiah 41:10

> He Himself has said, "I will never desert you, nor will
> I ever reject you." We can say with confidence, "The
> Lord is my helper, I will not be afraid. What can man
> do to me?"
> —Hebrews 13:6

> For God has not given us a spirit of fear, but of power
> and love and discipline.
> —2 Timothy 1:7

In such passages there is little compassion regarding our fearful plight. We tend to feel sorry for people in fear, but God offers no sympathy; He only gives clear commands. God takes fear seriously because it's unbelief, serious unbelief, a denial of the very nature of God Himself.

Fear is so serious that it is addressed over 360 times in the Bible, where we are repeatedly told, "Fear not." These aren't suggestions; these are commands. As Malcolm Smith pointed out, God is not offering condolences; He is saying, "No. Stop that. Repent." His words are given not to affirm us, but to correct us—a verbal slap in the face to break us of our trance and return us to the present. God is near; God is here. He is not only present in our surroundings, but alive in our spirits,[3] part of the great exchange that transpired upon us at the Cross.

With resounding defiance against the circumstances that trouble the heart, we are commanded to boldly declare the Truth. *"Rejoice in the Lord always... the Lord is near."*[4] If we concentrate on *not* worrying, we will be bound by it. Focusing on fear causes us to worry about our worrying, heaping fear upon fear with no end. Should we try to cease from worry without focusing on Truth, we will only multiply our troubles as we concentrate on things that don't exist. "You never go into a dark room and attack the darkness," says Smith.

Instead, we are to proclaim the Truth, and as Truth is illuminated again in the soul, fear has no place to hide.

Thus, the crippling problem of fear is neutralized by a single antidote: trust in God. In fear we deem that God is irrelevant. In trust we proclaim that God is essential, reality of the highest order. In trust we rebel against the lie and the imagined absence of God, joining in chorus with countless others who proclaim, "I believe in the Lord God Almighty, maker of heaven and earth, and in Jesus Christ His only Son our Lord…"

Trust comes from a deliberate and conscious choice to leave the imaginary domain where God does not exist and return to the present where God has promised that He will never leave us or forsake us.[5] Trust releases our burden of control and recognizes God's power over our physical destiny. It affirms the certainty of spiritual realities. In trust, "the peace of God, which transcends all understanding, will guard your hearts and your minds in Christ Jesus."[6]

The person without fear worries little of tomorrow, free today to be creative, active, productive in the here and now as the burdens of the future are entrusted to the only One capable of doing anything about them. No wonder Satan feeds our fear. No wonder the Dream Machine manipulates us by it. Those who trust are controlled by nothing but God's Word in their ear and His Spirit in their heart. They are free, free to love again, free to risk, and free to abandon all that has shackled them to the things of the world. Such people

> "When I know the love that God has for me, my mental confusion disperses like fog on a summer's morning."
> —Malcolm Smith

have found an empowering peace that not even death can contain. They are free to step into the unknown with nothing but God to catch them, for they know that that is infinitely more than enough.

A MOUNTAIN CALLED "SI"

The silhouette of the mountain continued to dominate the skyline above my home. I had been hiking for months, continually pushing further and further into the stress and into my fear. In calculated increments I pushed my body until I felt confident enough to begin to face Mt. Si. Picking reasonable daily goals, I chipped away at the ascent. After a month I had pushed my way up to the 1.3 mile marker… the next week I made it to mile 1.7, climbing 1,500 feet of vertical elevation. Progress, yes. But 4,000 feet above and many miles away, the summit seemed so, so distant.

Four weeks straight of traveling interrupted my progress. Back at home after weeks of inactivity; my legs were so out of shape that I decided to take a very easy hike up Mt. Si. *"Thirty minutes up, thirty minutes back. No problem,"* I thought. But at the trailhead, the ground moved beneath my weakened legs like the decks of a ship on the sea; my brain felt as if it were sloshing loosely in my head. It was hard to focus and difficult to balance, but I made it up to my goal in thirty minutes and stopped to rest and drink. I then decided to push it just ten minutes more.

As I walked up the steep trail, I prayed and focused on the two Bible verses that had accompanied me on so many hikes. A familiar cadence emerged again in my mind: *"The Lord your God is with you… the Lord is near…"* I was speaking to God as I always do on these walks… but then something happened that shocked me: His voice came to me, the voice of His Spirit resonating in mine:

"You will climb Mt. Si today and I will be your strength."

I knew immediately that the words were not my thoughts. The last thing I wanted to do that day was climb Mt. Si. It was way beyond any physical thing I could do at that time. *"Too high. Too far. Anything could happen,"* I thought. "Impossible, Lord. How do I climb the mountain? I didn't bring enough food or water to make the summit…"

"I took care of John the Baptist in the desert. I provided for the Israelites in the desert for forty years. I will take care of you."

It was a calling. It was my leap of faith. This was to be my test. The climb up Mt. Si encompassed every fear I had. 4 miles and 4,000 vertical feet, on steep trails through deep woods, inhabited by bears and mountain lions… it was more than I could do. What if I got hurt? What if I could no longer continue? What if I could not make the descent? *What if... What if... What if...?* But in the back of my mind, I heard echoes of the words I heard many months earlier, "You *will* climb Mt. Si." I had to obey.

I realized at that moment that I had never truly given 100% control of my life up to God. If I was to break free of my fear and live in God's hands, I had to climb Mt. Si. "Yes, Lord. I will climb," I said. My heart, however, told me this was madness. I knew what kind of shape I was in. I knew the size of the mountain. But I walked on, the steep switchbacks falling behind me one by one. In my fragile state I decided to hike as long as I felt okay. I thought I would commit to just two miles... but I passed the mark and continued upward. As I prayed up that mountain, my legs stabilized beneath me and my vision began to clear before me. A quiet peace soothed me from within. I was doing it! I was strong; I was feeling balanced on the narrow trail, finding my way again. I was going somewhere, pushing on through the clouds of doubt.

At 3,000 ft, fear began to catch up with me. Had I gone too far? What if I couldn't make it back? Had I passed the point of no return? On the edge of the trail I wrestled to regain my thoughts, praying with focused intensity for help and strength. The response came from within; words of sincerity that pierced my heart and challenged me to overcome all that constrained me: *For too long have I lived by fear. For too long have I lived my life through worry.* It was time to break through, to leave the past and the valleys behind and push on toward higher things. Inch by inch, foot by foot, Seattle dropped further and further below me, the trial leading higher and higher... until, that is, the path ended at a section of large boulders near the summit... boulders not unlike those of Joshua Tree.

A flood of images flashed through my mind... the feeling of being suspended, the pain ripping through my knee, the swirling blur of color, the cry of my daughter, helicopter blades cutting into the air... I stood facing the rocks. The air felt thick with substance... one of those moments when everything seemed so much more than physical, as if the stones and the sky were not of this earth at all... *Fear no evil, the Lord is with you... The Lord is with you... Fear no evil...* I put my hand to the rock and began to climb.

A few minutes later, I reached the summit and I looked out as the world stretched below in every direction. A huge smile came across my face and the burden of fears that I had carried for more than a year was lifted off my shoulders. God had called me to put my absolute faith in Him. I had failed the test so many times in life when I was at my strongest. But now, when I was at my weakest, I had put my faith in God. I did not fail; I climbed Mt. Si by His strength, not mine.

I realized at that moment that I can only have absolute peace in this world when I give absolute control of my life up to God. This is the way God intended it to be from the very beginning. And now seeing my world 4,000 feet below me, everything looked so small. The cares of our world, the things we worry about, the lies that invade our soul seemed so insignificant. All that mattered was walking in God's peace.

I was free at last.

Chapter 9

Inside the Dream Machine

Many are ruined by admirers whose heads are turned by the sight of a pretty face.[1]

—Socrates

The summer that I climbed Mt. Si was filled with monumental changes in all areas of life. Much of my journey out of the desert had been a blur and time itself was helping to bring clarity to much of what I had been through. Though I knew my vision was still very clouded I was capturing a clearer vision for the future as I pondered God, developed a clearer sense of self, and overcame the crippling oppression of fear. Spiritual realities were being integrated into the physical in my worldview, meshing together into a dynamic new paradigm for living.

The problem was that the lie still had a definitive presence in my psyche. Truth was permeating so many new areas, but the lie still had a hold on so many others. I thought I was free. I thought I understood. But I was mistaken. At that point, I'm not even sure I understood what the lie was. Thomas Aquinas, the passionate philosopher and theologian, once said, "For anything to be in the intellect, it must be first in the senses."[2] In order to see the lie for what it truly was, I needed to experience it on a sensory level. I needed to venture into the depths of the world that propagated the lie itself; I needed to go inside the Dream Machine.

And in the early summer I got my chance when I was invited to attend the world premiere of the new Charlie's Angels movie, *Full Throttle*. I knew this was a great opportunity—*Full Throttle* was one of the biggest movie releases of the year. I was about to enter Hollywood, the epicenter from which the shock waves of media radiated. This was the axis of so many of my aspirations, the genesis of so many dreams that had been shaped in my earlier years. Now I would have a chance to peek into the upper echelons of its structure, a real "back stage pass" to see what was going on behind the curtain, behind the cameras, behind the scenes.

THE RED CARPET TREATMENT

Walking into the glitter of the entertainment industry is like walking into a phenomenally different dimension in the Western world. Life moves differently, minds think differently, social patterns of the masses separate this population from the rest of the world. It's a subculture unto itself, where extreme affluence and opulence creates a unique and dazzling environment. The clothes, the cars, the buildings, the posture of those walking the streets; they are all in a league of their own. Under the warm glow of city lights illuminating the night and the warm rays of the Southern California sun by day, the Dream Machine never rests. Endlessly it churns out the continual stream of music, television, movies, and media that feed the world's appetites for information and entertainment.

The cadence in Hollywood moves to a predictable beat, a pulse of activity that surges humanity through the veins of the city. The rhythm reaches a crescendo when a studio unveils a new movie at a world premiere, as if the entire community is giving birth to a child of its own creation. The premiere itself is a carefully orchestrated balance of choreography and chaos, a blend of power and prestige mixed with the predictable mayhem of the masses who come to feed on the spectacle. Part celebration, part dedication, part corporate politics, and entirely promotional marketing, the premiere of a major motion picture is, in itself, a major production. When *Men in Black* premiered, Sony took over the Santa Monica Pier. When *Pirates of the Caribbean* was unveiled, the party engulfed Disneyland.

During a movie premiere the streets are lined with limos and exotic sports cars; movie stars, TV personalities, and rock 'n' roll icons come out by the dozens, trying to position themselves in the limelight as the paparazzi swarm about. It's all orchestrated to attract as much media attention as possible. Some studios will spend one million dollars or more on the evening of a premiere, knowing that it is one of their best publicity events.

Outside the theaters, barriers are erected to keep the press and spectators at bay. Thousands stand behind them, straining to get a glimpse of the rich and famous. Billboards and banners are carefully positioned as backgrounds for the paparazzi cameras, looking for the perfect angle to capture the perfect images.

Between the barriers, stretching from the street to the doors of the theater, lies a corridor—a thin line marking a definitive barrier between those that "are in" and those that "want to be." It's the red carpet and those who have "made it" to the top of the entertainment world walk upon it. The rest stand among the yearning, screaming masses on the street, dreaming of what it would be like to be on the other side.

That night I lived on the other side, I walked the carpet, I played in the game, and I loved it. The movie itself was good, but watching it in those theatres with all the fanfare and pomp… it was electrifying. After the movie, I again walked the red carpet, this time from Grauman's Chinese Theatre to the VIP party that was set up across the street. Six lanes of traffic had been blocked off; I walked down the center of the street between the barricades, as scores of fans and onlookers strained to catch a glimpse of their stars. Hordes of people were standing in reverent silence as we passed by. I wasn't someone worth seeing of course, but the allure of the attention was intoxicating, stirring desires from years gone by. Even after all I had been through, I was far from resilient to the ways of the world. I was tasting something new and it captivated my mind even as it enticed my desires. What the masses yearn for was being unleashed upon me in all its sensual intrigue. I was being swept away in the river of fame; I was touching what was out of reach, I was experiencing the dream of the machine.

Inside the VIP party, lights flashed, music played, and people moved around to see and be seen. My head spun from side to side as I saw faces—*real* faces—faces normally seen only in two dimensions on the television or the silver screen. Now they mingled about me in 3D.

On stage the Pussycat Dolls did their thing, moving with the music and leaving little to the imagination. On plush eight-person couches the stars (and those who had managed to get close to them) settled in to watch. Bruce Willis, Demi Moore, Ashton Kutcher, Cameron Diaz, Drew Barrymore, Lucy Liu, Sharon Osborne, Matt LeBlanc, and many more…

I was a nobody in that subculture, yet there I was in the midst of it all, stunned and breathless. I walked close to the couches to get a better view when Lucy Liu walked by. "How are *you?*" she asked. I opened my mouth but no sound came out. I just stood there with my jaw on the floor. It was pathetic. I'm the big businessman, I give speeches all the time; but this woman smiles at me and I freeze like I'm under a spell or something. I just stood there. She walked away, but looked back twice, probably thinking I was some sort of psycho or something. To regain a sense of control and shake off my daze, I started to walk around and shake hands with other stars at the party. I tried to meet as many as I could. When it was all over I collapsed in my hotel room… but not before making a list of every star I saw that night.

THE CALLING

Back in Seattle the healing of my soul and body continued. I continued to hike and climb; each outing a fresh blast of new air releasing my fears and restoring my soul. These hikes became a place of worship where I pondered God in the midst of His creation, walking step by step toward new horizons.

One morning I climbed to the top of a forbidding perch of rock called "Rattlesnake Ridge." At my feet a stunning 1,000 ft. cliff dropped into the lake below. The panorama was framed by the Cascade Mountains jutting from the horizon. In the valleys of the foothills, homes and buildings stretched toward the mountains. Cars, like small dots, wove their way through it all. From that distance humanity looked small and the cares of our world seemed even smaller. I spent some time reflecting on the journey that nearly killed me, that broke me of everything, and how I was now being rebuilt in the way God intended me to be. As I sat there realizing how far I had come since the accident, I began to feel God's presence with me.

I felt as I had when I was a child, seeking to serve God instead of my own pursuits. I had diverted my path for so long. My original intention to be a missionary to Africa was now but a distant thought. I had seen and experienced the world in so many ways—I was now a very different person than the one called to be a missionary to Africa. But the touch of God's plan on my heart felt the same as it had so long ago and it was as clear as the view below me. I was to reach out to the souls that were lost in this world, those who had bought into the same lie that consumed me and distracted me from peace and meaning in the world.

I knew them well. So many souls—so many like me—who had known God in innocence and had succumbed to a dual life of compromise—pursing the things of earth while praying for the things of God. And the countless others, those who had never heard of His graciousness and mercy at all, those still chasing the elusive dream, unaware of the inevitable emptiness of a world that promises so much and delivers so little.

The wind blew against my face, the sun warming my cheek. The childhood call I had received decades before was reignited. The past came together in the moment and I could see it all for what it was:

I had been created for a purpose from which I had wandered.
He had killed who I was so I could be used to offer rebirth to others.

My arrogance had been silenced so that He might speak.

God had saved me, then allowed me to suffer. Now He was in the process of forming me into something new, something usable.

I had died in many ways, only to be reborn to disperse the message of life.

I sensed God's plan washing over me in completeness: I was called to reach searching souls by sharing the story of what He had done for me in my journey. Something had been finished; something new was beginning; it was time to move on. Rattlesnake Ridge was not an end but a re-beginning, the start of a renewed journey.

The next week Sony Pictures called to offer me a position as a vice president. I would leave Microsoft and we would move to Hollywood to work for Sony Pictures. My thoughts raced ahead. "These are the people I am to reach," I thought. But I was wrong. I had a story to tell; I had things to show to others; but God was taking me to Los Angeles to show *me* something instead, something very important.

CALIFORNIA OR BUST

From a physical perspective, Hollywood really *is* all it's made out to be. It takes the best that the world has to offer, compacts it in a super concentrate, and then serves it to you through a fire hose in full force. You have to put up with smog, traffic, and the impersonal big city, but what you see from a distance is what you get. Power, pleasure, creativity, material possessions, and excesses all crowned with beautiful bodies and faces. It's unplugged and fully amplified all at the same time.

Everything in Los Angeles is over the top, including real estate prices. We tried to buy many homes in the middle of the LA real estate craze, but we were outbid every time, with the homes selling for up to one hundred thousand dollars over their asking price. We rented for a time and eventually found a home in Beverly Hills on Palm Drive, the same street Marilyn Monroe had lived on.

This was our new neighborhood. From this vantage point we had a great view to watch as the Dream Machine cranked out its magic. On the weekends, we would ride scooters down Rodeo Drive where tourists were always taking pictures of themselves. (No one else really went there except the few people who could actually afford to shop there—and wanted to be seen doing so.) When we took walks we would pass by homes owned by stars like Madonna, Peter Falk, and Ozzy Osbourne. When we went out to eat, we'd see the likes of Jeff Goldblum, James Woods, Jon Voight, and many others living out their daily lives, trying to be regular people outside of the media spotlight.

It was pseudo-normal, except for the fact that we were always on display. Buses full of gawking tourist drove through Beverly Hills all the time, their wide-eyed passengers marveling at the mansions, straining to see someone who was really someone. On our walks, Tiffany often wore sunglasses and a baseball cap pulled low, her long brown hair flowing behind. We also had this wimpy little dog that tagged along on a leash. Heads turned and out of state cars slowed, *"Look! Is she one of them? Is she somebody?"* I'd laugh as I walked behind her, watching the tourists gawk. For some reason they never gave me a second look; I guess my bald and dented head didn't rouse much curiosity.

On any given day, the streets were filled with fans who came to be impressed by the exteriors of the homes of the rich and famous, who hoped to catch a glimpse of life on the inside. They wandered here and there, heads turning in every direction. We were living in the proverbial human fishbowl, the whole world looking in. That was the point, of course: the lookers created the ratings; their monies fueled the machine; the machine churned out the dream the lookers embraced. It was amusing at first, this dazed stream of visitors who had come to the land of the stars.

In Hollywood and through Hollywood, Satan has created a world where God is absent and irrelevant, leaving a huge hole in the heart of humanity. In His place the media industry has created mini-gods, idols, golden calves of our own design to try to fill our innate need for worship. It was all very subtle and yet very blatant on the street. Hollywood isn't a place of media production, it isn't a tourist destination; *it is a place of worship*—a human cathedral where worshipers gather in droves to submit to pseudo-deities.

Those who came to worship in person—the tourists on the street, the fans behind the barricades—they came as pilgrims to the temples of the entertainment industry. They came exuberantly, yet insecurely—as if they were trespassing on holy ground. After all, this was 90210; this was what everyone wanted; this was the place where the gods lived. Like a Muslim to Mecca, like the devout Catholic in Rome, the reverence given was unsettling.

But in honesty, the gods themselves were not amused by the veneration and were annoyed by the petty adoration. Hollywood baited the world, but in reality the residents were also the prey—and they resented those who leeched off of them, sucking the normalcy out of daily life.

INSIDE THE MACHINE

Behind the doors at Sony Pictures, my work fell into a regular corporate routine. Lunch time, however, was anything but typical. My office was next door to the Sony Pictures production lot, a city unto itself consisting of over twenty sound stages. It is one of the most famous and historic production sites in the entire world; the place where movies like *Gone with the Wind* were brought to life. This was where the Dream Machine did its work, just as it had for dozens of years. At noon I would go to the lot, grab something quick to eat and walk the streets of this strange world—this place in between ideas and the screen where visions were created, ready to be sent into the minds of the masses.

From day to day, I never knew who or what I would see. In one sound stage I would see the TV show *Wheel of Fortune* being produced, then I'd walk around the corner and see the movie *Zathura* being filmed. Sets were always being built and then torn down as fast as possible to make room for the next movie. Some of the sets were amazing. Intricate and convincing, they created their own little world in the chasms of the cold concrete buildings. The Machine had all the tools it needed to create any dream, but there was nothing "real" about any of it. The back side of the two-dimensional sets revealed them for what they were; false façades based only on appearances.

The stars would walk from set to set, not unlike business men and women on a city sidewalk or a carpenter on his way to a construction site. On the lot, sheltered from the gawking tourists and admirers, the actors moved freely and unpretentiously, able to be themselves, able to be the humans that they are. Day after day I saw that the only thing that makes "stars" different than anyone else is their tremendous ability to pretend to be someone else within those sets. With the help of lights, makeup, costumes, computers, props, and media networks that span the globe, the actors are on the frontlines of the mirage of the Dream Machine. But behind the scenes I came to appreciate them as humans and as artists, skilled professionals portraying false identities. It's not reality and it certainly is not some sort of moral compass by which we should direct society.

REAL LIFE?

Off the lot and away from work, family life in Beverly Hills existed somewhere between the façade and the genuine. There were places and moments when normal Americana seemed to dominate and in those times we'd feel a brief sigh of normalcy. One of those places was the soccer field where our kids played in the Beverly Hills Soccer League. But even at soccer games, we were always reminded of where we were.

One day I met Val Kilmer on the sidelines. Of all the stars I saw at work and in Beverly Hills, he was the only one I just had to introduce myself to… and I'm glad I did. Val was a kind and gracious man. We talked about muscle cars, soccer, our sons, and how old we were beginning to feel. "*Top Gun* was twenty years ago. Can you believe it?" he said with a smile. "I guess that makes you over forty," I laughed.

Being around him seemed so natural and yet so odd. I was standing next to the actor who had so vividly portrayed my idol, Jim Morrison, in the movie *The Doors*. Val, the actor, had been instrumental in shaping the direction of my wayward years. But that day

Kilmer, the dad, was just like me. Maybe there was something real to this after all.

On the days Tom Cruise and Katie Holmes showed up at the soccer field, dozens of paparazzi were always in tow, toting cameras with huge lenses, trying to get the inside scoop through the fence. One weekend as my kid's soccer game ended, I sat in disbelief watching the swarm of paparazzi take pictures of Katie at the soccer field. Soon after, I saw those same pictures end up in the tabloids. The paparazzi destroyed any semblance of normality. In some ways it was a show—a chance to get publicity—but I knew it came with a price. They were prisoners within society, never free from the public eye. Where could they go when they needed to be real? Did they even remember what being a mere human was like? As I walked freely with my children, I felt sorry for them and the bondage in which they were captive.

Tiffany was never as wide-eyed about the whole scene as I was. She viewed it all with both amusement and annoyance. She thought it was all interesting enough but really took a "Yea, so what?" attitude. (She's so strong. The glitter of the world has never captured her heart like it has mine.) Still, I couldn't shake certain impressions from my thoughts, a growing sensation of hollow feelings that encompassed most of what I saw.

On Sundays, we attended church at the Oasis Christian Center in an old converted movie theatre in the heart of Hollywood. Famous actors and rock stars regularly attended. Just like other churches, some would come to worship and enjoy the company of others who believed. Others came inside looking for a sanctuary from the craziness of life outside.

Others who came to "check out church" were at the top of the industry, having achieved their fame through the darker sides of entertainment. Looking for alternatives to the crass and demeaning identities they had created for themselves, they seemed to be looking for a way to redefine who they had become. The tension between their heart's desires and the demands of their careers, however, was intense. They had created an act and then they were unable to escape it. The momentum of the Machine created great pressure on them to continue performing. They were torn between two worlds and most of them wanted both. They were... well, they were a lot like me. And just like me, they were facing two choices. They could either turn toward God or live out their own self-imposed realities, prisoners in a jail of their own design.

BEHIND THE CURTAIN

In the neighborhood, at work, at the world premieres, and in church my preconceived notions and my expectations were being greatly challenged. A paradigm shift of major proportions was taking place in my mind. I was wresting to see clearly, trying to conceptualize a new way of seeing the entertainment world and myself as fresh impressions were merging in my worldview.

The paradigm made a significant shift the night my wife and I went behind the scenes at the MTV movie awards. We knew that anyone who was anyone would be there; hundreds of stars surrounded by their agents, friends and handlers; screaming fans on the red carpet; and a worldwide TV audience in the millions.

We made our way to the backstage area where limousines were lined up one after the other, dropping off the stars and their entourages hidden from the views of fans. You could feel the surge of energy through the cameras and the crowd. Star after star primped and prepared themselves for the masses that waited screaming on the other side of a curtain where the red carpet would lead them inside.

But something felt different this time; it struck me much differently than the *Charlie's Angels Full Throttle* premiere had. At first I couldn't put my finger on it. Something was simultaneously affirming and yet disconcerting. Was it real or was it surreal? It was tangible to the senses, but to the heart it was void of substance. Perhaps I was finally waking up.

The whole situation seemed to be a strange mixture of needs and desires and positioning and feeding. The commodity of fame was somehow being exchanged and traded and everyone wanted their share. The paparazzi circled like sharks closing in on wounded fish, searching for that perfect candid image for their editors. TV cameras in the wings offered the world a glimpse of the world behind the lights, but not too much, just enough for the viewers to think they had seen something special. The stars acted as if they were above it all, but of course they needed it all as much as anyone.

Somehow, those cameras were the conduits of everything everyone wanted. A strange flow of give and take transacted through the lenses that connected this strange world to the masses in the television audience. Everyone needed it, ratings depended on it, marketing depended on it… this was one of the crucial moments where everything in the free-market of the mirage all came together at a crucial point. Everyone had a part; everyone played the part perfectly; everyone's dream depended upon it.

We eventually left the hustle of the red carpet area and made our way to the backstage door where we sat down and watched the spectacle from behind the scenes. That night, almost everyone who was on stage came and went through that door; the presenters, the award winners… everyone. Queen Latifah, Uma Thurman, Jimmy Fallon… it was an endless mix of the leaders in the entertainment world. Now and then a backstage camera would come out to get candid shots. One major star and his entourage passed through the area, but the cameras were turned the other way. I watched as he slowed down and positioned himself to get their attention, but the moment the cameras focused on him, he briskly moved on, pretending to be indifferent to the exposure.

When the cameras left, however, the mood shifted significantly and I began to see the Machine from a different angle: it was the red carpet without the carpet; it was life behind the curtain when the lights were aimed elsewhere; it was a snapshot of human reality… and it looked intriguingly *normal.* With the cameras gone, some of the stars laughed and conversed at ease, comfortable with where they were and what they were doing. The faces of others, however, fell into disconcerting and uncertain expressions—a graphic contrast to the confidence they portrayed on stage. Some looked bored and agitated. Cigarettes dangled from the nervous fingers of others. A few seemed to fall into a haunting trance of passive annoyance. Everyone around us had made it to the top of the top. They had achieved what we hold in the highest regard and within their hands they held everything the world had to offer. So why the vacant, empty stares? Were they wondering if they had the right things? As a group, did they have anymore peace or meaning than the crowds on the other side of the barriers? Had they found any satisfaction in the success? It didn't seem like it. In many ways some seemed far more lonely and empty.

For a moment the veil lifted and I could see beyond the physical. I was standing with them in the midst of their own personal deserts. They had followed the mirage to this place seeking meaning and peace. From a distance it all held such promise, but up close the visions had evaporated. They were left standing on dust, dust at the very spot from which the pools of clear, satisfying waters had appeared. The contrast was so striking. Here they all were, in Hollywood, able to indulge in everything the physical universe has to offer, worshiped and adored by the masses. I was standing among the living legends, but the place we were standing was dry, lifeless, and void. The only ones who were at peace seemed to be those who were indifferent to the physical illusions of this place; those who had found peace and meaning elsewhere.

That night, behind the scenes at the MTV awards, the Dream Machine was revealed for what it is—just another mirage deep, deep in the same desert shared by each of us. It's a machine and it's a dream. It's art and it's fiction. For some reason, society has made gods of those in the lights, but when the cameras turn the other way, the gods become human once again—and many of them are fearful and guarded, just like the rest of us.

I had again made it into the inner sanctuary of the world's holy place and that night I pondered where I fit within it. I intrinsically knew that I was a stranger to this place, a foreigner in this world. Something *was* different, something *was* out of place—and it was *me*. I knew what my soul hungered for and I now knew it was not to be found in the midst of this illusion where joy and peace ricocheted between the buildings, finding no place to rest in the hollow void of human hearts.

Behind the curtain the mirage had evaporated before my eyes, revealing the universal, tainted longings of humanity. We're all the same really; deep inside we're all vulnerable to the lie. Without God's grace and the life-giving breath of His Spirit, our lives would be uncontrollably swept away by our desires for comfort, for possessions, for attention, for power. Satan and the world so gladly dangle these temptations before our hungry hearts today; so carefully baited, so full of promise, yet so empty in the end.

As the evening progressed, Tiffany and I looked on with a strange mixture of intrigue, amusement, and sadness. The dream had been revealed for what it was, a false utopia at the pinnacle of success's illusion. When it was over and the frenzy of the crowds died down, I wrestled with a growing disillusionment. Everything that I thought was so cool had turned out to be just another hollow shell, a physical shadow, void of meaning and peace.

In the months that followed I spent much time reflecting on my own life, even as I tried to make sense of theirs. In Hollywood I found real people—not "real" in the sense that they were free to be themselves, but real in the sense that beneath the thick veneer they were authentically human. Like all of us, they were trying as best they could to get what they thought they wanted, but just like any other worldly pursuit without God, it turned to dust in their hands.

It was a sad, sober realization. But like any truth that finds its place in the human soul, it was freeing. The way of Truth was replacing the way of the lie. The shackles of the lie had finally fallen from my ankles. The Dream Machine had been exposed for what it is and I was free to walk into the future and explore the road ahead with new clarity, new purpose, and new direction.

Chapter 10

The Road Ahead

We move about the earth with unprece-
dented speed, but we do not know, and
have not thought where we are going,
or whether we will find happiness there
for our harassed souls. We are being
destroyed by our knowledge, which
has made us drunk with our power.
And we shall not be saved without
wisdom.[1]

—William Durant, 1929

O n October, 2005 my wife, my dad, and I returned to Joshua
Tree—my third trip into this forbidding place and first trip back
since my incident three and a half years before. Twenty years ago I
had come as a child and wandered in youthful innocence. The second
time I had come as a family man on a picnic—and departed in a flurry
of blood, dust, and helicopter blades. Both Tiffany and I had vowed
to never return to Joshua Tree; we were ready to leave behind the dark
feelings and memories associated with the place. In time, however,
God gave me the desire to return one more time. As we drove through
the desolation of the California high desert, we knew in our minds
that there was nothing to fear—but it took faith to proceed and we

were glad to have each other by our side. Tiffany was apprehensive; my dad was curious. I wasn't sure what to feel. I had come for a sense of closure on this latest season of my life; I desired to face the place that had set me on such an incredible journey; I hoped to understand the miracle in its true context.

As the car doors slammed shut, the hush of the desert descended like a blanket. The shifting of the rocks and sand beneath our feet broke the stillness as we moved from the parking lot toward the rocks jutting from the horizon. It was dry; it was stark; and the familiar beauty still radiated from the bareness. The hike along the desert floor was longer than I had remembered—or could it have been that I just had much more to remember now? Tiffany was to be my guide that day, showing the way into the past, and she was the first one to recognize our destination. "There," she said. "That's the cliff; that's where you fell."

In the shadows of the cliff, memories of the accident became alive again—clear visions of what had taken place so long ago. Approaching the rocks, we stood for a moment at the base, taking in the setting. Then Tiffany began to move from rock to rock. She moved like a choreographer retracing the steps of a fragmented dance. "This is where we were huddled. That's where you were with Jake." And 45 feet below that spot, "Here is where you landed. Your head was like this; your legs twisted like this. I can't move my arm like yours was…" She tried to be careful, but the abrasion from the rough stone cut into her skin. It is no wonder why the rocks shredded me the day I fell from so high.

We talked in matter-of-fact tones as Tiffany pointed out certain features of the landscape. I asked questions; she corrected some of my distorted memories. The sequence and location of other details found their appropriate place in my thoughts. As she talked, sounds of the past echoed in my mind: the screams of my daughter, the uncertain words of comfort from Tiffany, the crackle of radios, and the voices of the rescuers…

We talked in detail, but when there was nothing else to say I decided to sit quietly on the spot where my life had been so changed; the place where it should have ended. The profound implications of what had transpired there led me into deep introspection. Three and a half years had passed. Three and a half years of pain, suffering, perseverance, hope, and understanding. I had learned so many things since my journey began in blood on this rock:

1) MIRACLES HAPPEN

During the self-absorbed college years and the early years of business success, I felt I held my destiny in my own hands. I lived and thought independently of God, certain that I was the master of my own fate. But looking at the scene of the fall, I knew I was sitting at the scene of a miracle, a place where God had directly intervened and altered the course of physical events around me.

Since the fall, my rational human mind had wrestled with doubt. Was this a true miracle or just a chance fluke? Standing at the spot where it actually happened, however, verifying the location and height from which I fell and the way I landed, I came to two unavoidable conclusions: First, I could see no natural explanation for the accident; there is no physical reason I should have fallen at all. Second, there was no question that I would have been a dead man had God not intervened between me and the rock. I tried to contort my body into the same position that Tiffany had found me in. I tried pressing my flesh into the crags. I tried to twist my limbs as they had been, but it proved painfully impossible. When I considered the momentum from falling 45 feet onto those same unforgiving rocks, I imagined what *should* have happened: I could visualize my skull cracking, my pelvis shattering like broken glass, my shoulder ripping apart. All things considered, it was impossible that I could come away with just 35 stitches, a stapled knee, and a bad concussion. I should have immediately died with many parts of my body twisted and broken. Like the ranger had said, "Drop 100 people off that, and 100 die."

It *was* a miracle. By God's grace and intervention I had been saved; I was alive; and now I was a very different man than I was before. A wave of humility and gratitude flooded my soul. God *is* alive and active in the physical realm. Miracles occur. God transcends the perceived physical/spiritual barriers at will—and such movements of God are to be expected and accepted.

2) TRUE REALITY EXISTS IN THE SPIRITUAL WORLD

Unlike some, I find no honor in my past. There is no glory in the days when I partied without the concern of sin and embraced the lies of this world. I was deceived, I was a fool, and I left a lot of damage in my wake. I was a success only at compartmentalizing God in a dualistic worldview; I excelled only at denying His reality in the affairs of everyday life. As I pondered the transformation that had happened in my life since the fall, it became clear that when I fell over the edge in Joshua Tree, my beliefs were catapulted over the edge as well. For the first time in many years I had seen that the spiritual not only *permeates* every aspect of life, but that the spiritual actually *defines* life. The physical is only a shadow. I now recognize that my earthly struggles are but reflections of a spiritual war that rages. Everywhere I turn I see the physical effects of spiritual sin. I now know that unless I incorporate the spiritual as the most tangible aspect of my being and existence, I shall forever be deceived, never to see reality clearly.

And if you think about it from the perspective of eternity, it is the spiritual that is real and the physical that is the fantasy.

3) THE DREAM MACHINE THRIVES ON THE ILLUSION

Looking back, I'm amazed at my ignorance of my own worldview and my inability to discern from where it had come. My philosophical wanderings had mixed with my pride and I was completely blind to the vulnerability of my soul. I thought I was so smart and so independent. Instead I was a naïve puppet, out of control and manipulated by the superficial insinuations of Hollywood. I can see it so much more clearly now; the pervasive influence of media is a dominant force in our culture, molding our thoughts, expectations, and choices.

The car accident after Joshua Tree was my initial wake-up call, opening my eyes to the illusion of the Dream Machine. Previously, I embraced certain elements of media entertainment as if they were my ideal reality; I conformed my life to their values, dreams, and behaviors. At the same time I was buying into the images of success peddled by the advertisers who bombard us with 163 billion dollars in marketing each year.[2] It had never dawned on me that they were trying to sell me more than a car—they were manipulating me by creating an ideal picture of who I needed to be and what I needed to have to be successful and significant. Again, I followed their lead and conformed to their desires. Joshua Tree, the ensuing car accident, and the years I spent in Hollywood shattered the illusion.

4) THE JOURNEY IS ESSENTIAL, INDIVIDUAL, AND ONGOING

While I would like to think that I've become a master of certain truths, I know that I am still very much a student—a sojourner who is finding his way out of the lies of the world, the devil, and my own desires. The great lie of the material world is constantly telling us that meaning and peace come from the things we have, the way we look, and the things we do. I know in my mind that this life is not what it seems, but in my human heart I am still drawn to the false illusions of this world. I still attempt to drink at the deceptive and dry mirages that offer only superficial satiation of my thirsts.

I am so very, very grateful for the truths that have guided my journey from the desert of lies. I had sought the meaning of life in the things of this world, walking on the razor's edge every day. It was inevitable that my worldly life would come crashing down. I am thankful that my crash came as early as it did; so thankful that no more days were wasted in the fog of the illusion; so thankful that my life was spared.

I'm convinced each of us must walk through this desert at some point in our lives. I wish that my words and my advice might save you from the pain and suffering that is required to die to self and be stripped of the lie, but that is not possible. I can only offer comfort and insight from my journey and perhaps add perspective and hope to yours. There is no route around the desert. There is no shortcut through it. In the desert, we face the reality of our insignificance and our weakness. In the sands we find the humility that allows us to begin to see God more clearly. During the journey, God uses pain and suffering to guide us and heal us, allowing it to shape and refine us according to *His* purposes rather than according to *our* desires. Philosopher Viktor E. Frankl said:

> Even pain and the death of desire find their place in light of the eternal purposes. Suffering ceases to be suffering in some way at the moment it finds a meaning, such as the meaning of sacrifice… a man's main concern is not to gain pleasure or avoid pain, but rather to see a meaning in his life. That is why a man is ready to suffer, on the condition, to be sure, that his suffering has a meaning.[3]

As I sat on the rocks that day and gazed into the desert before me, my personal journey found fresh meaning and I fathomed the infinite value of the journey itself. My godlessness had led to my demise; my ego had required that I be crushed. I deserved so much more than I got. I had justified my sin with the help of the images and ideals projected from the entertainment world. Satan had attempted to destroy; yet God had used it to heal and restore. In this literal and figurative desert my lies were exposed for what they were. Eventually the pain allowed me to be set free from the lies of worldly bondage. In the end, God gave me what I had searched for and never found in this world: the peace that surpasses all comprehension—and it is worth every drop of blood and sweat I put into the journey.

5) THE ABSOLUTE FORGIVENESS OF GOD IS REALITY

Each of us brings with us a past—a past full of ignorance and indiscretion that leaves us morally polluted and guilty before the holiness of God. The human psyche is rightly burdened by the oppressive weight of this guilt, yet God Himself provided the way out… He offers forgiveness. Each of us, by God's grace, can claim the biblical promise that "If we confess our sins, He is faithful and just to forgive us our sins and cleanse us from all unrighteousness."[4]

For as long as I can remember, I have known the forgiveness of God. It was a precept of my childhood Sunday school experience; in my Christian junior high, forgiveness was assumed and common place. I took forgiveness for granted as my path went the way of the world, as I allowed my soul to be consumed by lies. Before the fall, I had reveled in my independence, thinking I was able to accept the consequences of my sin.

Through my fall, God has changed the entire paradigm through which I contemplate forgiveness. I knew *about* forgiveness, but the morning after the accident, when I stood in front of the mirror, I felt it... I *felt* absolute forgiveness. I saw my guilt for what it was and I saw that it had been entirely washed away. It was a simultaneous awareness of the full weight of my sin *and* the reality of the sacrifice Christ made on the Cross. I cannot explain it nor can I define my experience without it. Forgiveness is divine justice and infinite love... it's the amazing grace of God poured out on one so entirely undeserving. In some obscure but entirely tangible way, I saw that I had died; I was looking at a newborn baby in the mirror. My life was a clean chalkboard, erased of my past, ready for God to write a new life.

I've tried to communicate that feeling of absolute forgiveness to many people. Most react with a combination of jealousy and unbelief. In our culture—particularly in our Christian subculture—we are shackled by our guilt. We are willful prisoners of our past and present—and we are often fearful of future judgment. Is it that we cannot comprehend this kind of forgiveness? Are we unable to fathom this kind of love and sacrifice? Is it our pride that clings to a false sense of self-righteousness? Does our sense of economy insist that we can (and must) somehow earn this type of divine favor? Is it our defiance that keeps us from broken honesty with God, making us unwilling to accept His lavish forgiveness?

I don't know. All I know is that I don't deserve the forgiveness of God. Yet I felt it the day after the accident looking at my battered body in the mirror. I felt it still, three and a half years later as I sat on the rocks where my journey had begun. The absolute forgiveness of God is a reality; His grace is amazing and eternal.

6) TRUE PEACE AND MEANING ARE FOUND IN GOD AND GOD ALONE

As I sat on the rocks pondering all that had happened, I was struck by another truth that I had denied before the accident but had since come to believe from the heart: God is good; God is in control; and He is the only One who can fill the emptiness of the fallen human heart. In Him alone can we find that which is so deeply desired by each of us: true peace and meaning in life. Moment by moment I have the opportunity to place my faith in God in every circumstance, to be anxious for nothing, and to continually give thanks as I make my requests known. When we go to God, we will continually and repeatedly discover what we are looking for in substantial measure. It's not just an option—it's an imperative: a nonnegotiable blessing for the one who desires to live in freedom and Truth.

In those times when my faith falters, when I go to the world to fill the inner longings of the soul, I place myself at the mercy of chance and circumstance. Should I follow this path I will continually walk on the edge of fear, often falling into the abyss of stress, anxiety, and panic. Should I go the way of the world, the peace of my soul is ever dependent on the fragile, decaying circumstances around me. Faith and fear are mutually exclusive and the choice between them is up to me.

In order to learn this lesson, I had to experience decades of empty searching, a near death experience, a miracle, and years of pain and suffering. Now I know that God alone is worthy of my submission, my worship, my trust. All else is but a temporary surrogate, an unsatisfying substitute for the peace that is found in Him—the peace that is embodied in a relationship with the Creator through Christ.

7) THE DAYS AHEAD DEMAND DISCERNMENT AND DEVOTION

There was a time when I allowed life to cascade at random, guided only by momentary whims for pleasure. Now I can't escape the fact that there is a plan for my life. I believe that God has prepared a way in which I am to walk. I'm convinced that He has an appointed purpose and a mission set aside for each of us, a way of living that we are to pursue for His purposes.

Yet it seems so contrary to reason: why would God choose the likes of me and the likes of you for a holy and eternal purpose? In and of myself, I know that I am nothing, that I am inadequate, that I am a failure. Like the Apostle Paul (who at one time assisted in the murder of God's followers) I would consider myself to be "the very least of all saints.'" Yet as I sat on the rocks, I felt a confirmation in my heart that I have been destined for something—that we are *all* destined for something.

As I search the Bible I've found that God is accustomed to using people like me. I join the ranks of the liars, adulterers, deniers, who find nothing in themselves worthy of service to a King such as God. But by pondering God and who I am as His child, I can boldly proclaim that "without God I can do nothing,'" but "I can do all things through Christ who strengthens me.'"

As such, the future holds tremendous potential for good, for evil, and for compromise between the two. The will of God stretches before us like a path along the ridge of a high mountain; a trail that leads to heaven along His intended route. Divergence from the way of God's intent can lead to eventual or immediate destruction. Every step of the way, alternate paths lead down into the valleys or to the edge of cliffs—like veins slowly flowing down into darkness.

By ignorance, arrogance, and indifference I had once found myself so far down, so deep into the shadows, that the path of God's intent seemed entirely out of view, impossible to return to. But even this was a lie. We have the promise of God's mercy (should we be willing to receive it), which returns us to His intended path as we heed the continual call of His unconditional love. We may feel we've diverted too far, but there is no pit so deep that the love and forgiveness of God can't bring us home.

With a clearer understanding of both the physical and spiritual implications of obedience and discernment, we are now compelled to choose between the things of God and the fleeting things of the world. Choices must be made at every intersection. The choices are not "maybe;" they are "yes" and "no," and each one matters. One must contemplate where each choice leads, insignificant as each might seem, for one-by-one each decision determines the course of our days between now and the grave.

Daily we must navigate through the invisible battle, attacked by foes that we cannot see. Between today and death, we are left with choices. We must decide between investing and trusting in the things that cannot and will not last or the things of eternity that will never fade away. We may feel alone on the path, yet we travel with Christ—the only one who walked the road perfectly, never once veering from God's intended path. It is His Spirit that fills us; our lives are now His life and He can be trusted to do the very work that He has prepared for us to do. Though deviations from God's intended path will be a continual reality, we have the ability, through Christ who lives in us, to walk straight ahead into God's unfolding plan.

With these new possibilities comes an unusual but important responsibility: to ponder God. The moments we spend in focused awareness of His presence and His Truth will be multiplied back to us in many ways. Above all things, it is intimacy with God that will keep us in His intended path.

While His peace can fill our lives with calm, a sober sense of urgency exists as well, for our time is limited upon this earth; the end to our journey is a certainty. As I pondered what had transpired in Joshua Tree, I knew that God had spared me from death. But soon enough, physical death will become my reality—just as it will for all. This was something I had understood at a young age, even though I avoided its implications. The summer before my senior year of college, I visited the National Gallery of Art in Washington DC, walking alone amongst its statues and paintings. My journal reflected stark impressions from what I saw:

> The myriad of statues glared upon the face of the inquisitive youth. What did the youth see? A time gone by where each man had his own dreams, his own destiny. What remains of their search for glory?

All of their aspirations entombed in granite and marble. Their voices silenced. And the people that once praised their achievements are gone…

Face upon face, of man preceding man. Glorified to other men by oil on canvas. As the painting fades, so does the memory of their existence. No man is immortal. No life is guaranteed.

Yes, death is an unavoidable future reality, a cloud that looms over a horizon an unknown distance away. Before Joshua Tree, the grave was only theoretical. I knew in my head it was certain, but in my heart I still felt the immortal, indestructible optimism of my youth… another lie to be refused. Death can come at any moment; we walk this earth for an incredibly short period of time, infinitesimally short actually, when compared to the eternity that awaits on the other side.

To walk in wisdom on this earth we must somehow come to grips with this mortality, but there is no room for despair. To the one who has embraced the love of God and accepted His forgiveness, death is the ultimate gateway to peace and meaning. Plato once said, "So long as we have the body… we shall never attain completely what we desire."[8] When we die, we will step out of the physical and our eyes will finally see spiritual reality in vibrant purity. No longer distorted by our worldview, we shall gaze with perfect clarity into Truth. For so long we have sought an integration of the spiritual into the physical. When we die, the physical will be left behind and we shall be absorbed into an eternal spiritual place where God is experienced in His fullness forever.

This is the road ahead, the road that began in the desert and ends on the threshold of eternity. I've come to know how the road begins and by faith I know where it ends. As for the details of the journey? God alone knows what lies ahead. We are the painting; He is the artist. We are the book; He is the author. God transcends our existence and defines what was, what is, and what is to come. In God we can trust. To Him we release control. He is the answer to life's question.

> *Lead me to the water of life, O Lord. Cleanse me of all earthly woes; and may my spirit proclaim to all that peace is found in You, that You are the bridge which leads to Yourself, that all mankind may cross.*

◆　◆　◆

I sat for some time on the rock in Joshua Tree reflecting on these things. The blue of the sky and the faded hues of the rock formed an appropriate backdrop for my thoughts. It was such an unusual place, such an odd setting for such life-changing events. For a few moments, as I gazed across the rocks and sand, I saw it all for what it was and for what it wasn't. Joshua Tree was just a stage, a prop in one scene of my life. The events that had transpired there were no more. An act had been played out in this place for a handful of fateful hours and then time had moved on.

As I sat I felt the indifference of the rock beneath me—uncaring, unrepentant of what it had done to my body. It was, after all, just a place—a place where a journey had begun. It was just an end, a beginning, a death, a rebirth… it was a blindness followed by sight… that's all.

As I pondered it all, a peace that matched the expanses of the sands on the horizon welled up in my heart; a consummation of all that had happened and all that was ahead. *"Go forth with confidence,"* God spoke in the stillness. *"Go forth with confidence."*

Quietly we walked the trail back to the car. With the rocks shrinking in the rearview mirror, there was one more thing to ponder: "Joshua Tree." "Joshua" means "God saves." Early settlers had named these trees for their outstretched limbs that gave them shade and hope as they journeyed westward across this vast land. I couldn't help but think that this place has saved me even as it nearly killed me.

Dad, Tiffany, and I talked more as we left the park entrance, but our conversation was cut short when the cell phone came alive.

Tiffany tried to recover more than a dozen messages, but reception was still spotty. Something was wrong; something had happened. We called home but through the poor signal we only gathered three things: *Jake. Terrible accident. Hospital.*

We drove; we prayed; we were stunned. Behind the stainless steel doors and under the florescent lights we found our ten-year-old son, Jake—bloodied, shaken, and scared. Tiffany scooped him into her arms, recalling what she saw:

> *It was like a flashback. He looked like Paul did after his fall. The scrapes, the blood, the staples in his head... His injuries were not as severe as Paul's, but they were so similar. It was spooky. They looked so much alike.*

Jake was bruised and battered, but he was okay. I let out a sigh of relief—relief that receded into anger and then grew into resolve when the details of the accident were recounted: At the *very* moment I stood on the rock where I had fallen and received God's call to "Go forth with confidence," my son's body was being twisted, crumpled, and cut in a golf cart accident in my parent's neighborhood—another freak event that defied reasonable explanation. He had been hurt, but not as bad as he should have been when the cart rolled his body beneath it. Was this just a coincidence? What was I to think of the "accident"? Was this yet another "miracle"? What did this mean?

There were no clear answers, but as we held each other in the midst of the chaos, tears, blood, and pain—I realized that we were experiencing something beyond the physical turmoil around us: we were experiencing spiritual peace—a peace that superseded circumstance and understanding. That's when I knew for certain that my family had all been changed by Joshua Tree—both that day and in all the years since. We'd come to embrace the fact that we will face trials and tribulations on this earth. There *is* a battle that rages across imagined lines between the physical and spiritual, and we will have our share in this struggle until the day we breathe our last.

But far and above that fact is the reality of God, the God who exists in the here and now. He is holy and good, deserving of our full confidence and trust. He is also in control and He is faithful, worthy of our submission and obedience. If we trust in Him and if we follow Him, He will guide our steps and protect our hearts. Though our bodies will meet their eventual demise, in God we shall have the peace and meaning we seek.

Jake would recover from the "accident" without complication, but we look back on that day with both humility and thankfulness. Fear was defeated. Joy was ours. God had proved Himself more than sufficient for us. We left the hospital with renewed clarity and determination:

> *In this life we will share laughter and tears, mountain tops and valleys, deserts and death. It matters not what comes our way as long as we have found God and choose to walk with Him according to His ways.*

Such is my life; such is your life. Such is life *over the edge*.

Endnotes

Introduction
1. George Barna, *The Invisible Generation: Baby Busters* (Barna Research Group, 1992).

Chapter 1
1. Nietzsche, Friedrich in Tim Hansel, *You Gotta Keep Dancing* (David C. Cook, 1998), 32.
2. Revelation 12:7, 9, 17

Chapter 2
1. TV-Free America Television and Health <http://www.csun.edu/science/health/docs/tv&health.html> (Accessed 5/19/2008)
2. Thoreau, Henry David <http://www.brainyquote.com/quotes/quotes/h/henry-david132662.html> (Accessed 5/19/2008)
3. 1 Samuel 16:7
4. 2 Corinthians 4:16

Chapter 3
1. Douglas, Norman in Tim Hansel, *Holy Sweat* (Word Publishing, 1987), 54.
2. Stephen Glenn, Jane Nelsen, *Raising Self-Reliant Children in a Self-Indulgent World* (Three Rivers Press, 2000), 25.
3. World Advertising Research Center, Data <http://www.warc.com/LandingPages/Data/Adspend/Adspend-ByCountry.asp> (Accessed 5/19/2008)
4. Will Durant, *The Story of Philosophy* (Simon and Schuster, 1961), 236.

Chapter 4
1. Eliot, T.S. <http://www.brainyquote.com/quotes/quotes/t/tseliot109032.html> (Accessed 5/19/2008)

2. Buechner, Frederick in Tim Hansel, *You Gotta Keep Dancing* (David C. Cook, 1998), 19.
3. James 1:5
4. Ecclesiastes 2:3, 4, 8, 17
5. 2 Corinthians 11:3

Chapter 5
1. Pascal, Blaise <http://www.brainyquote.com/quotes/quotes/b/blaisepasc39550 8.html> (Accessed 5/18/2008)
2. Tim Hansel, *You Gotta Keep Dancing* (David C. Cook, 1998).
3. Pope, Alexander in Tim Hansel, *You Gotta Keep Dancing* (David C. Cook, 1998), 31.
4. Will Durant, *The Story of Philosophy* (Simon and Schuster, 1961), 246.
5. Mencken, H. L. in Douglas Soccio, *Archetypes of Wisdom* (Wadsworth Publishing Company, 1998), 259.
6. Jeremiah 29:13

Chapter 6
1. Friedrich Nietzsche, *The Gay Science* (Vintage Books, 1974), 181.
2. A.W. Tozer, *Knowledge of the Holy* (Harper San Francisco, 1978), 1.
3. Douglas Soccio, *Archetypes of Wisdom* (Wadsworth Publishing Company, 1998).
4. Summa Theologica, Basic writings of Saint Thomas Aquinas, (New York: Random House, 1945), Part 1, question 2, article 3.
5. Fred Heeren, *Show Me God* (Day Star Publications, 1998), xix.
6. Michael Behe, *Darwin's Black Box* (Simon and Schuster, 1996).
7. Randal Keynes, *Darwin, His Daughter, and* Evolution (River-head Trade, 2002).
8. Pascal, Blaise <http://www.brainyquote.com/quotes/quotes/b/blaisepasc39550 8.html> (Accessed 5/19/2008)
9. Voltaire in Douglas Soccio, *Archetypes of Wisdom* (Wadsworth Publishing Company, 1998), 260.
10. Genesis 3:1-5

11. Lewis, C. S. in Fred Heeren, *Show Me God* (Day Star Publications, 1998), xix.
12. Albright, William in Fred Heeren, *Show Me God* (Day Star Publications, 1998), xviii.
13. Einstein, Albert in Douglas Soccio, *Archetypes of Wisdom* (Wadsworth Publishing Company, 1998), 249.
14. Hosea 6:3
15. Galatians 2:20, Peter 5:7, Matthew 6:26, Romans 8:33-39, Ephesians 2:4
16. A.W. Tozer, *Knowledge of the Holy* (Harper San Francisco, 1978), 98.
17. Psalm 46:10

Chapter 7
1. Will Durant, *The Story of Philosophy* (Simon and Schuster, 1961), 251.
2. Thoreau, Henry David <http://www.brainyquote.com/quotes/quotes/h/henrydavid132662.html> (Accessed 5/19/2008)
3. Ecclesiastes 1:2
4. Genesis 3:3
5. 1 Peter 5:8-10, Revelation 12:7-9
6. John 1:14
7. John 1:17-18 THV
8. John 14:6
9. John 19:30, 1 John 1:9, Acts 16:31
10. Galatians 2:20, 1 Peter 3:18

Chapter 8
1. 1 John 4:18
2. Eliot, T. S. <http://www.brainyquote.com/quotes/quotes/t/tseliot161678.html> (Accessed 5/19/2008)
3. 1 Corinthians 6:19, Galatians 2:20
4. Philippians 4:4
5. Hebrews 13:5
6. Philippians 4:7

Chapter 9

1. Socrates in Douglas Soccio, *Archetypes of Wisdom* (Wadsworth Publishing Company, 1998), 79.
2. Aquinas, Thomas in Douglas Soccio, *Archetypes of Wisdom* (Wadsworth Publishing Company, 1998), 226.

Chapter 10

1. Will Durant, *The Mansions of Philosophy: A Survey of Human Life and Destiny* (New York: Simon Schuster, 1929), pp. vii, viii.
2. World Advertising Research Center, Data <http://www.warc.com/LandingPages/Data/Adspend/Adspend-ByCountry.asp> (Accessed 5/19/2008)
3. Viktor E. Frankl, *"Logotherapy and the Challenge of Suffering,"* in *Psychotherapy and Existentialism: Selected papers by Viktor E. Frankl* (New York: Simon and Schuster, 1967), 90.
4. 1 John 1:9
5. Ephesians 3:8
6. John 15:5
7. Philippians 4:13
8. Plato in Douglas Soccio, *Archetypes of Wisdom* (Wadsworth Publishing Company, 1998), 310.

Paul Jensen is a business executive, father of two, and husband of 15 years. He and his family currently live in the Seattle, Washington, area.

To learn more information please go to **www.pondergod.com**

Printed in the United States
203453BV00003B/178-639/P